The Awakening Human Being

A Guide to the Power of Mind

Barbara Berger

With Tim Ray

BOOKS

Winchester, UK
Washington, USA

First published by O-Books, 2011
O-Books is an imprint of John Hunt Publishing Ltd., Laurel House, Station Approach,
Alresford, Hants, SO24 9JH, UK
office1@o-books.net
www.o-books.com

For distributor details and how to order please visit the 'Ordering' section on our website.

Text copyright: Barbara Weitzen Berger 2009

ISBN: 978 1 84694 835 0

A CIP catalogue record for this book is available from the British Library.

Design: Stuart Davies

Cover photo: Søren Solkaer Starbird

Printed in the UK by CPI Antony Rowe
Printed in the USA by Offset Paperback Mfrs, Inc

We operate a distinctive and ethical publishing philosophy in all
areas of our business, from our global network of authors to
production and worldwide distribution.

The Awakening Human Being

A Guide to the Power of Mind

Other books by Barbara Berger

The Road to Power
– Fast Food for the Soul

The Road to Power 2
– More Fast Food for the Soul

Gateway to Grace
– Barbara Berger's Guide to User-Friendly Meditation

Mental Technology (The 10 Mental Laws)
– Software for Your Hardware

The Spiritual Pathway

Are You Happy Now? 10 Ways to Live a Happy Life

Single for the Second Time
– The Adventures of Pebble Beach

Other books by Tim Ray

Starbrow
– A Spiritual Adventure – book 1

Starwarrior
– A Spiritual Thriller – book 2

101 Myths About Relationships That Drive Us Crazy
– And A Little About What You Can Do About Them

CONTENTS

Bonus Tracks

Introduction

What are you seeking?

What is it you want more than anything else in the world? Ask yourself and answer truthfully. Answer as if it was the night before Christmas and you were a little kid and could have whatever you wished for. Take out a piece of paper and write down your answer, your honest answer. You don't have to show this to anyone else—this is just for you—for your own enlightenment.

OK.

Now what did you answer?

The reason I'm asking you this question is because we (my son Tim Ray and I) have been holding lectures and workshops in many countries… and we often start by asking the audience this question.

And the results are always very interesting.

After everyone has written down what they want on a piece of paper, we ask people to share. And this is what they say.

One person answers, "I want to have a good relationship." And then we ask the person "Why do you want to have a good relationship?"

And then the person usually answers, "Because I want to experience love," or "because I want to feel safe and secure." And then we ask, "Well why do you want to experience love or feel safe and secure?"

And the person will say, "Because it will make me feel good." And then we say "And why do you want to feel good?" And then the person will say, "Because then I'll be happy."

Then we'll take the next person who wrote, "I want to have a job where I can use my creativity and talent." And then we ask, "Well why do you want to have a job where you can use your creativity and talent? What will that give you?"

And the person will say, "Because it will give me a feeling of satisfaction to use my creativity and talent." And then we ask, "Well why do you want to feel satisfied?" And the person will say, "Because then I'll be happy."

And then we'll ask another person and she will say, "More than anything in the world, I want good health. I want to be strong and healthy." And then we ask, "Well why do you want to be strong and healthy?" And the person will answer, "Because then I will be able to do what I want." And then we'll ask, "Well why do you want to be able to do what you want?" And then finally the person will answer, "Because it will make me happy."

And so it goes... It's a very interesting experiment (please try it yourself and see what you discover). We've discovered that regardless of what people say they really want, if you ask them why they want what they want – be it health, money, a good relationship, good sex, loosing weight, having healthy children, being creative, world peace—whatever it is—it's always because they believe that these things will bring them happiness. And yes, everyone wants to be happy. Everyone is seeking happiness. Everyone, in every country, of every age, weight, height, sex, background, wants to be happy.

You could say happiness is the universal drive. It's the same for everyone – we all want to be happy. And all the things we seek—whatever they are—we seek them because we believe that if we attain what we seek, then we'll be happy.

If you don't believe this is true—ask the people you know. Ask them what they really want (in their heart of hearts) and then ask them why they want whatever it is they really and truly want. And you will find, if you keep asking, that everyone, without exception, wants what they want because they believe it will make them happy.

Even if we're seeking enlightenment—or the way out of suffering—we are doing so because we believe this will make us happy.

But how?

So the big question, of course, is how do we experience the happiness we seek? Why aren't we happy right now? What is preventing us from being happy right this moment? Why do we believe we need to achieve or obtain things in the outside world to be happy? Why do we think the right partner, a good job, losing weight, having nice kids, being healthy, having money in the bank, or world peace will make us happy?

This is the big question—the eternal question. How do we achieve the happiness we seek?

Another way of saying this is—how do we put an end to suffering in our lives and in the lives of others?

This is man's eternal quest.

The way out of suffering.

The way to happiness.

* * *

I have been searching for the answer to this question all my life— and all my books deal with this question.

One of the things I've discovered is that most people are looking for happiness in the wrong place. They are looking for happiness in the outer world (in the world around them) and they believe that by attaining some of the things we just mentioned—the right partner, a good job, nice children, money, a nice house, success, a fit body, etc. they will be happy. But when you think about it, isn't this the cruelest belief? Isn't it being very cruel to yourself to believe that your happiness depends on outside circumstances, people and events? Especially when all the things we're talking about are things we have absolutely no control over. What could be worse? What could be more difficult to achieve when there is absolutely nothing out there in the physical world that you can depend on to live up to your impossible expectations? (Not to mention the fact that we live in a world where so many people, in fact most people, will never have most of the things we believe are necessary for happiness!) And yet this is what we are all doing when we believe our happiness depends on finding the right partner, getting a better job, earning more money, having the perfect body, the perfect house, the best designer furniture—or whatever it is… It is utter madness and cruel to boot.

So why are we doing this to ourselves? Why? How did we get like this?

As far as I can see it's because this is what we were taught. Our parents and teachers taught us this and we believed them. And why did they teach us this? Because this is what they were taught and so they taught it to us—all in good faith of course. And we, in our childish innocence, we believed them. We believed our parents and teachers because this is what innocent children do. Innocent children believe the stories they are told and that's what we did. So we believed that yes, our happiness *does* depend on outside circumstances, events and people because this is what they told us. And most of us still believe this. Most of us still believe that the right partner, more money, power, so-called security, and/or a healthy body will ensure our happiness and keep us safe from this thing called life. This is the teaching we all receive, so it's no wonder most of us believe it without question.

And as a result of this belief, we try so hard to obtain all of these outer things to make ourselves happy until sooner or later most of us find out that there's something wrong with this teaching—because it doesn't work. Either because we don't get the things we think we need to make us happy—or because we *do* get most of the things we think we need and we're still not happy! So sooner or later we get pretty disillusioned…

And then some people, when they've suffered long enough and are unhappy enough long enough because of all these crazy beliefs and all our crazy expectations, may start asking what's wrong? They may start asking why isn't this working for me? I've been so good and I've tried so hard, why don't I experience the happiness I seek? What am I doing wrong? What's wrong with me?

And then when this type of existential despair really hits home, some people actually wake up and discover their old belief system doesn't work because it has nothing to do with reality. Their belief system doesn't match reality, which can be a pretty big shock. They find that when they really look at reality—*at what is*— that reality isn't like their beliefs at all. Reality is quite different even though it's always been there— right before their eyes. They just didn't notice.

> This is what we mean by "Getting Real".
> We mean waking up to reality.

So what is this reality I'm talking about?

Well to begin with, the reality is we live in a world of impermanence and each and every one of us is born with a changing physical body. And the thing about physical bodies is that sometimes they get sick and they all age. And this goes for everyone. So right here (just for starters), we find that believing a perfect body and perfect health are the key to happiness must obviously be the direct route to hell—because it's never going to happen. And I don't mean you shouldn't do everything you can to live a healthy life, what I do mean is that even if you are super fit and healthy for a good many years, the reality is that *all* bodies do age—no matter what we do. And everyone dies—sooner or later.

Another thing we all discover (again sooner or later) is that no matter how hard we try—we don't always get what we want or what we think we need to make us happy. That too is reality.

So we discover that what we were taught—that our happiness

depends on other people, on getting what we want, on the right circumstances, on good health just to name a few—is the direct route not to happiness but to unhappiness, fear and anxiety, misery and depression.

Reality is what it is

The truth is no matter what we do, reality is what it is and we don't have a choice. It's not in our control. It is what it is. Life is what it is. One day it rains and the next day the sun shines. Do you have any control over that? You are breathing and your heart is beating, do you have any control over that? Events and people appear before us and then they go away. Do you have control over that? Parents, partners, children, friends all come and go and things happen and life moves along quite on its own—do you have any control over that? And there you are, with this particular body, doing all the stuff you do until the body gets sick or breaks down, or gets old and the breathing stops and the heart stops beating. And that too is the way of it.

So what does any of this have to do with your expectations? Sometimes life delivers what you think you want and need, and sometimes it doesn't. But if you really watch what is going on, it becomes pretty obvious pretty fast that you're not the boss. No matter how hard you try, life does what it does and you're not in control. And it doesn't matter how fit you are or how much money you have in the bank, reality is what it is and you're still not the boss.

That is the way of it.

And as for partners, it's the same. Sometimes we have nice partners and friends and sometimes we don't. And when it comes to money, well sometimes we have money in the bank and sometimes we don't. And that too is the way of it. Just look around you and you will see that this is true for everybody. There are no exceptions to reality. No exceptions.

So obviously, *obviously*—believing that you need a partner, health, money in the bank to be happy is not the way to happiness! Why? Because when you base your happiness on these things—on these impossible expectations—you are fighting reality. You are asking for the impossible. You are expecting reality to deliver what you want and chances are that's not going to happen—ever. So this way of thinking, the way we've been brought up to think, everything we've been programmed to believe is in fact the direct route to hell. And I repeat—the direct route to hell and not to happiness. Why? Because life is what it is. Reality is what it is. We're not running the show and we don't have a say in the matter. This moment—the real—is what it is. And that's final. It's done.

But again please don't misunderstand me here. When I say that reality, this moment, is what it is, I don't mean you shouldn't live sanely and work for change or work to create a better world. I don't mean you can't do everything in your power to live a good, sensible, kind life. I don't mean you shouldn't develop your wisdom and understand the law of cause and effect and how it operates in your daily life. No I'm not talking about that. What I am talking about is the fundamental nature of our experience of living this physical existence with these bodies. I'm not talking about all the wise and practical steps you can take to live sensibly in this world with these physical bodies or the many wonderful things you can do to help your fellow men and women. What I am talking here about is our *unrealistic expectations* to this thing we call life and how these *unrealistic expectations* lead us straight to hell. So it's better to wake up to reality and understand the nature of this thing we call life, because when we understand this, we *can* live happy lives. It is possible. And this is the good news.

In fact, this is very good news.

Why? Because when you look deeply into the nature of this thing called life and begin to understand what life is and the way the mind works, you will come to realize that in fact your happiness does not depend on any outside circumstances, events or people. This is the core realization. This is the heart of this understanding. When things begin to fall apart and then you begin to see what's really going on, you will discover that the happiness you seek is an internal event, an internal experience. And that this internal experience has nothing to do with all the things you were programmed to believe your happiness depended on! And this is why I say this is the good news... because it means you're free! You are free! Your happiness doesn't depend on anyone or anything... *It's up to you. And there is something you can do about it!*

Take a moment and ask yourself

Let's look at this from another angle for a moment. Ask yourself what is actually preventing you from being happy right now, right this very moment? If you are honest with yourself, you will probably say it's because you don't have what you want. You will probably say that the only thing that is preventing you from being happy right now is wanting something you don't have. This could be better health, a partner who's more understanding, more money in the bank, or a nicer apartment, or a million and one other things. But whatever it is, it's something you don't have at this very moment in time. And this is what's making you unhappy right now. Isn't this true? Isn't it true that you're unhappy right now because you feel there is something you are lacking?'What else could possibly make you unhappy at this very moment? It can only be the thought of what you don't have. Because what else is there? You are sitting here right now, reading this book. And what's wrong with that? The only thing that can be wrong with this moment is your own dissatisfaction with what is. It has to be this because there is absolutely nothing else is going on. And this brings us to the crux of the matter which is *all our experiences — every single experience we are having — is just a thought in our minds.* There is reality — in other words what is—and then there are your thoughts about what is going on—and this is your experience. That's all that is going on. You're sitting here, reading this book. Nothing else is happening. And you're either liking what's going on or you're not liking it. And that's always the case and this is always true for all of us. We live and things happen and then we think some experiences are good and other experiences are bad or at least less good. We live and things happen and then we think the experiences, events and people live up to our expectations or they don't. And that's what we get to live, that's our experience. It's as simple as that. There is nothing else going on.

It's all just thoughts in our minds.

Always. All the time.

Just look at your own experience. Either you are thinking you like something or you are thinking you dislike it. And that's about it. The situations in themselves, the specific events, circumstances and people are just what they are. In and of themselves, they have no inherent value. We can like them or we don't but they're still just what they are. Our preferences don't really have much to do with it at all. Life is unfolding before us, for us, and everything we see, hear, touch, taste are just the happenings of being alive. It's our preferences that make us happy or sad.

The truth of the matter is there is reality—and then there's our thinking. And these are two different things.

Reality check: How to take care of your own thinking

Nobody has ever taught us how to take care of our own thinking. And this makes us suffer immensely because we think that our suffering comes from Life itself. (But Life doesn't send suffering, Life just is.) Nobody has taught anybody how to take care of their thinking because

> nobody knows how to take care of their thinking…
>
> We all believe that what we think is true and this is the cause of all our suffering. We never learned to distinguish between our thinking and reality.

Radical stuff

Now I know this is very radical stuff but it's true nevertheless. And this brings us to the startling conclusion that you and I can lead happy lives regardless of our circumstances, regardless of what we have or don't have. Because when we drop our interpretation of events, we find ourselves living here and now in this present moment. And that's about it. With no stories, no comparisons, no expectations, life just is and we are just here. And what could possibly be wrong with that? And so we find, to our great and eternal delight, that at this very moment, when we drop our stories and beliefs and stand quietly in the now, we're quite happy! We find that right this very moment everything is ok. And that strangely enough, happiness is what we are. Happiness is our nature, our natural state.

But what exactly is it about the present moment that makes this so? The great paradox is that the moment you step out of your stories—even for just a minute—the radiance and amazing power and presence of the now shines through. A radiance that is beyond the comprehension of our thinking because it is beyond our thinking. And we find that this radiance, this awesome power and presence, is our true nature.

And it's all so very delightful because when we stop trying so hard to achieve and are simply present, there is a peace that is joyful, free and which is precisely the happiness that we all seek—beyond time and space, beyond thinking and mental constructions, beyond our personalities and life stories and expectations and dreams. When you discover this and experience this for yourself, you find that the *suchness* and richness and presence of this moment has been here all along. We just didn't notice it. And the only thing that was hiding this radiance from us was our own non-stop mental chatter and expectations. We were so busy with all our stories, comparisons, thoughts, beliefs and expectations that we missed the power and the presence and the radiance of life right now.

But even if we don't notice it, this radiance never goes away. Regardless of how attached we are to our identities and stories, this radiance and peace is always present. So the moment we drop our stories and step into this now moment we find that we are radiantly happy right now — and for no apparent reason at all!

This is the magic of life!
And it was here all along.
We just missed it!

Now I know we have all been brought up to believe otherwise, but I'm here to tell you that what you learned is not true. You may believe that your happiness depends on your health, on outside circumstances, on your good looks, or on the amount of money you have in the bank, but it's just not true. Your happiness depends on nothing because you are already the happiness you seek. You are this, all of it, this moment! Now!

And this means you can live a happy life regardless of outside circumstances because without all your thoughts and expectations, without the thought that you "need" something to make you happy, you will discover the unconditional happiness, the radiance and joy, that is your innermost nature. It might take a while for you to find this out, but when you do, you will see that this is the most wonderful, liberating and absolutely lovely discovery you can possibly make. Because it means you are free! It means you can live a happy life right now, whatever your circumstances are. It means that happiness has nothing to do with health, money or success. In fact it means that happiness has nothing to do with anything outside of you at all.

And once you get this, once you really see this and get your realization, you will truly understand why I say that nothing external can influence your happiness one way or the other unless you allow it to. You can only experience your own thoughts.

> Happiness is what you are.

The way the mind works

So now you understand why this whole book and all my other books are about the nature of consciousness and the mechanics of how our minds work. Because it is here you will find the key to your own happiness, the key which will set you free—regardless of your circumstances. So read the material in this book carefully and contemplate it every single day of your life.

If we can see and understand the mechanics of consciousness and the way the mind works and how this shapes our lives, we will find the key we've been looking for. And it's not a mystery. Understanding the way the mind works is a matter of impersonal law. It's something everyone can observe. And this means it's something you can observe and test for yourself. So check out the things I write about in this book and see for yourself if they are true or not.

Consciousness is the precondition

Before we dive into the way the mind works and look at what I call the mental laws, it is important to understand the context in which all our thinking (all mental activity) is taking place. All mental activity takes place in the context of what we call consciousness. Consciousness is something we all have—or rather are—right now, right this very moment. Right now, right this very moment, you exist and you are conscious. You must be or you could not be reading this book. Existence or consciousness is the precondition to everything, to every experience. Consciousness or awareness is the background upon which everything (both mental and physical) unfolds and takes place. Consciousness is a prior to all experiences or happenings. Consciousness is the infinite field of awareness, the Ultimate Reality, the context in which all content arises and disappears. And as we shall see, all mental activity is the content which arises and takes place in this infinite field of awareness which is what we all are. Without consciousness, we could not experience this thing we call life. I mention this here because later in the book we will also be looking at the experience of being present in this moment beyond the changing landscape of all our thoughts... but for now we are going to look at how our minds work. We are going to look at the mechanisms that govern the way our thinking shapes our lives.

Law is unchanging principle

To start, I'd like to consider the concept of impersonal law because just as there are physical laws that describe the way phenomena operate on the physical plane, so there are also mental laws or principles that describe how our minds and mental phenomena operate.

So let's start by looking at the concept of impersonal law.

What is a law? A law is a principle or we could say a description of an impersonal phenomenon. Webster's Encyclopedic Unabridged Dictionary of the English Language defines a law of science as "a statement of a relation or sequence of phenomena invariable under the same conditions..."

In other words, a law is an impersonal sequence of events that is not dependent on the person or people involved in that sequence of events. In addition, laws can be observed and confirmed by anyone. Here are some examples of physical laws:

The law of gravity: The law of gravity is an impersonal law and is always operating. According to this law, if a person jumps off a 10-story building, he or she will immediately fall to the ground. There are no exceptions to this law or principle. It doesn't matter if you are the President of the United States, a cashier at the local grocery store, a famous pop star or you. It doesn't matter if you are having a good or a bad day. It doesn't matter if it's day or night or what the weather is. The law doesn't stop working just because it's Christmas or your birthday. The law is impersonal and operates regardless of the situation, time of year, or the people involved. This means the law doesn't stop working and say, "Oh I think I'll make an exception here because little Mary has been such a good girl this week. I don't think she deserves to hit the ground and break her neck." Since laws are impersonal, the issue of deserving doesn't enter into the equation.

Another important thing about a law is that it is in operation whether you are aware of it or not. In other words, if you jump off a 10-story building, you are going to fall and hit the ground whether you know about the law of gravity or not. So again, you can't say after you jumped that you didn't realize you would fall and hit the ground if you jumped. The law doesn't take your individual level of awareness or preferences into consideration. The law just operates; it is a blind force of nature.

The law of sowing and reaping: The law of cultivation, of planting seeds and harvesting a crop, is another good example of a physical law. Every farmer knows that if he plants potatoes, he's not going to get strawberries. He knows that the type of seed he plants determines the type of harvest he can expect. He knows if he plants cabbages, he won't get roses. And he doesn't expect otherwise. He doesn't take this fact personally because he knows it's an impersonal law.

The other important thing a farmer knows is that in order to harvest a crop, he must plant something first. In other words, he can't harvest something from nothing. He must plant seeds first, which leads us to another interesting law.

The law of cause and effect: Just as a farmer knows he must plant a seed in order to harvest something, he also knows that nothing comes from nothing. In other words, a farmer doesn't expect to get something out of nothing. There has to be something to produce something. There must be a seed before a plant can grow. This means that in order to have something, something must cause it to happen. We call this the law of cause and effect. The law of cause and effect says you cannot have an effect without a cause. If you want to harvest radishes, you must plant radish seeds first. You cannot harvest radishes from thin air. There must be a cause to have an effect.

Another important aspect of this law is that the effect always has the characteristics of the cause. In other words, the effect is the result of the cause. So a farmer knows that if he harvests radishes, he must have planted radishes. A farmer doesn't go around saying, "...the reason I am harvesting radishes is because I planted strawberries." In other words, we can determine the nature of the cause by examining the effect, because we know that they must have the same characteristics.

Another good example of a basic law or principle that most people are familiar with is:

The law of color: Everyone who has been to Art School knows that there is a law that governs colors. When, for example, you mix blue and yellow, you always get green. Again it doesn't matter who you are or whether you're having a good or a bad day, when you mix blue and yellow, the result is green. You are not going to get red, no matter who you are or what you do. Again, this is because the law governing the color spectrum is an impersonal physical phenomenon. It is something that is always true and was always true. It's not something that just suddenly went into operation because you started going to Art School.

This brings us to another important point.

Laws have always existed

Physical laws, such as those described above, have always existed. They didn't just suddenly happen or begin operating because someone discovered them. They have nothing to do with our level of intelligence or how aware we are. For example, the people who lived in ancient Babylonia 4500 years ago (2800-1750 BC) could have had cell phones and computers at that time because the physical laws upon which our modern technology is based were in existence then too. The only difference between today and the time of the Babylonians is that apparently the people who lived then did not know about these laws. If they had known about these laws, they could have had computers and cell phones, too. But just because they were unaware of the laws governing physical phenomena, it doesn't mean that these laws didn't exist at that time.

Let's take another example: the phenomenon we call electricity. According to Webster's Encyclopedic Unabridged Dictionary of the English Language, electricity is "... the fundamental physical agency caused by the presence and motion of electrons, protons and other charged particles manifesting itself as attraction, repulsion, luminous and heating effects, and the like..." This physical phenomenon has always existed. But since the Babylonians didn't have electric light, we can also presume they were unaware of the phenomenon even though it was there. And since they were unaware of it, they could not harness it and direct it to their advantage. We had to have great geniuses like Benjamin Franklin (1706-1790) and Thomas Edison (1847-1931) who could first describe the phenomenon and then explain how to utilize this mechanism before mankind could begin to direct this force of nature for everyone's benefit.

The same is true of what I call *mental laws* — the laws which describe the way our minds work.

Mental laws

Just as there are physical laws that describe and govern the behavior of physical phenomena, there are also mental laws that describe and govern the way our minds work. And again, these laws can be observed and confirmed by anyone.

Simply because most human beings are not yet aware of these mental laws and how they operate, it does not mean that they do not exist. Mental laws do exist. And since they exist, they must exist now and be operating right here and right now, whether we are aware of them or not. And not only that, since they are laws, they must have always existed.

Throughout history, there have been people who have known about these mental laws. In fact, the study of metaphysics as well as much philosophy and religion is an attempt to explore and describe these mental laws.

One thing, however, is quite certain: The study of mental laws is not yet being taught in our schools anywhere in the world. But it should be and I believe it soon will be. Everywhere we go and teach this—people always say "Why didn't we learn this in school? It would have saved me so much trouble if I'd only known all this before." So yes, the study of the way the mind works and the mental laws can dramatically change our lives.

Characteristics of laws

Laws are invisible principles.

Laws describe how phenomena behave.

Laws operate automatically.

Laws are impersonal.

Laws don't take sides.

Laws operate equally for all.

Laws don't care who you are.

Laws don't care if a person is "good" or "bad".

Laws are always operating.

Laws operate whether or not you are aware of them.

Laws are mechanical.

Laws are indifferent to the outcome.

Laws operate for individuals, groups and nations.

Laws are scientific*.

*Science is the study of natural laws that are impersonal and can be observed, confirmed, and used by anyone. Science can be defined as the observation, identification, description, experimental investigation and theoretical explanation of phenomena.

Using mental laws wisely

Another interesting thing about the discovery of mental laws is that once we recognize their existence, we can start using them wisely. The laws governing electricity had to be discovered before this power could be directed for the benefit of mankind. The same goes for mental laws. These laws must be recognized and understood before we can harness this power for the benefit of all mankind.

Software for your hardware

The application of mental laws is what I call mental technology. You can compare understanding and applying mental laws to having the right software for your hardware. As you know, it doesn't do you much good to buy a fancy, new computer and put it on your desk. To make this high-tech piece of equipment work for you, you must have the right software. Without software, your hardware is pretty useless.

If we apply this analogy to you, we could say your hardware is your mind. Now everyone has a mind, but before you or anyone else can use your mind effectively and harness its power for your own and other people's benefit, you must have the right software. Understanding mental laws is the software. With this knowledge in hand, you will be better able to run your mind. In other words, you will understand the mechanism and you will be better able to direct the power of your mind in the way you want.

At present, not many people have the necessary software, i.e., the understanding of mental laws, which is required to make their hardware (their minds) work wisely for them.

* * *

So with this in mind, let's take a look at what I call mental laws...

PART 1: PRINCIPLE

THE MENTAL LAWS /
THE WAY THE MIND WORKS

LAW 1: THE LAW OF THOUGHTS ARISING

Thoughts arise and disappear

Thoughts arise and disappear. This is the first law because it describes an impersonal universal phenomenon which is true for everyone. No one knows why or where thoughts come from or what a thought is, but everyone has thoughts. This is the nature of life on this plane.

You can observe and confirm this for yourself. You can test this and see if this is true or not—for you.

Here's what to do.

Look at a white wall

Sit down on a chair and face a white wall. If possible a wall that is completely blank—with no pictures or anything—just a plain white wall. Preferably there should be nothing specific on the wall for you to look at. Now sit down and look at the wall and decide *not to think*. Decide to make your mind blank. Try to do this for two minutes. Just sit there and look at the wall and do not think. Can you do it? Probably not. Why not? Well because thoughts arise. That is what happens. Thoughts just arise. And you can't make this not happen. You can't make your mind go blank for very long because thoughts suddenly appear—and seemingly completely of their own accord. Obviously it wasn't you who made the thoughts come. Especially since you decided when you sat down on the chair that you were just going to sit there and look at the white wall and *not think*. But you couldn't, could you. Why? Because it's just not possible—it's not possible

23

for anyone. And this is not because you were doing anything *wrong*. No not at all. It's because the nature of life on this plane is that thoughts just appear all by themselves. This is the nature of mind. It has nothing to do with us. We are not making thoughts happen.

Thoughts come and go on their own.

That is why this is a law. It happens to everyone. It's an impersonal phenomenon. And it's something you can observe and confirm for yourself.

And it is happening all the time—to everyone—in every waking hour of our lives.

If you watch very carefully, you can even see it happening. If you sit quietly for a while, you can actually see how a thought just arises—and you can look at it for a moment. And then what happens? Well then the thought disappears again. All by itself. You didn't do anything in particular and still the thought just goes back to wherever it came from—wherever that was. And then what happens? Well if you're still sitting quietly and looking at the blank wall—you will notice that another thought arises. Again, all by itself. And all you were doing was just sitting there in the chair, looking at the wall and trying not to think!

So now you know. *Thoughts do arise and disappear*. This is the truth; you have observed it for yourself. You have tested this for yourself and you can see that this is actually happening for you. You can see that thoughts *do arise* in your mind and that they *do disappear again*. And the interesting thing is that this is going on all the time. Even when you're not sitting and staring at a blank wall. And you're not willing this to happen. In fact you have nothing to do with it at all. The fact that thoughts arise and disappear again is a completely impersonal phenomenon. It just happens. And there's nothing you can do to stop it either.

What about meditation?

But what about meditation you ask? Lots of people meditate and many meditate because they want to calm the mind and stop thinking. But does this happen? Is it possible?

Well in my experience, you can't prevent thoughts from arising. Even people who have meditated for years can't *not think*. It is true though that when you sit and meditate, you do calm down and the thought stream does slow down. But what you also notice is that when you sit and meditate and observe, thoughts still arise and disappear. Maybe at a slower rate, but the thoughts still arise and disappear again. This is something you become very aware of when you meditate. And you can sit and sit and watch them come and go.

And of course as you get more experienced at meditating, things do slow down and yes, you may have less thoughts arising and you may also identify less with them and not get so attached to them anymore. But still thoughts arise. You may not find yourself going off into stories and getting lost there for a while. But still thoughts do come and go. You may also experience so-called "gaps" or spaces in between the thoughts because they come more slowly, but thoughts are still happening. The reality is thoughts continue to arise and disappear again because this is the nature of mind.

So if anyone tells you that meditation is about not-thinking, don't believe them. Try meditating regularly yourself and see what happens. (For more about meditation see Part 2 page 106).

LAW 2: THE LAW OF WITNESSING

There is a difference between you and your thoughts

There is a difference between you, the one who is having thoughts, and the thoughts themselves. This is another impersonal universal phenomenon and is also true for everyone. Once someone has pointed this out for you, you can observe this and confirm it for yourself. (This is why it's a law; you don't need a Ph. D. to see this...). So yes, you can observe that there is a difference between you and your thoughts. And again you can test this for yourself. So how do you do this?

Back to the white wall

To test this law, go back to your chair facing the white wall. Now sit down again and look at the white wall and just breathe and see what happens. The same thing will happen that happened the last time you sat down on the chair and looked at the white wall—thoughts will arise and disappear. But this time I'd like you to notice something else. I'd like you to notice who or what is watching the thoughts arising and disappearing? Who or what is observing this phenomenon?

Immediately when I ask you this question, you notice that *you* (whatever that is) *are watching the thoughts arise and disappear*. So obviously you cannot be the thoughts that are arising and disappearing—since you are watching them come and go! *You* (whatever that is) are there as the thoughts arise and *you* (whatever that is) are there as the thought disappear again. So there must be a difference between you and the thought since *you* (whatever that is) are still there once a thought has disappeared again. So you cannot be the thoughts that come and go. No, you are something else. You must be the one that is witnessing, watching and observing. You must be the witness, the watcher, the observer. Watch closely what is going on as you sit there looking at the blank wall and you will see that this too is true— that there is a difference between you, the observer of the thoughts, and the thoughts themselves.

Notice you are still there

When you begin to see this, you will see that you (the witness) are always there whether you are thinking "this is a good day", "this is a lousy day", "I have a cold," "I'm feeling wonderful", "I'm depressed," "I'm angry", "I'm tired". It doesn't make any difference what thoughts (and feelings) arise, you are still there. You, the witness, the one in whom the thoughts are arising and disappearing in. You are still there.

This is a very important, fundamental discovery, so please test this for yourself until you are completely convinced that *you* are not your thoughts. Observe and confirm this phenomenon until you can see the difference between the one who is observing (*you*) and the thoughts that come and go.

The key to freedom

This discovery—that *there is a difference between you and your thoughts*—is so important because it is the key to freedom. This basic discovery will open the door to great insights, greater understanding, and in the end—total liberation from whatever is bothering you. So please remember this and think deeply about this law.

Now why do I say this? Well for many reasons, but mainly because most people today are still totally identified with their thoughts. They think *they are their thoughts* and thus they are run by their thoughts—often leading to untold suffering and disastrous consequences. But when you begin to wake up to the nature of reality and realize that there is a difference between *you* and your thoughts—it allows you to step back and examine your thoughts instead of being run by them. And not only does this give you a little space and a little more distance to the things that are happening in your life, this discovery can actually lead to the birth of wisdom! Or you could say this discovery is the birth of wisdom! And the key to freedom! Freedom from the tyranny of your own thoughts and beliefs and freedom from the tyranny of what you perceive to be other people's thoughts and beliefs! That is why this discovery is truly transformative!

But again—don't believe me. Just keep on testing the concepts that I present in this book and find out for yourself whether or not they are true. Once you have ascertained for yourself that they are true—they will begin to work their magic in your life.

Reality check: Content versus context

We can call the observer in which thoughts arise *context* because the observer is the field in which thoughts appear and disappear. Thoughts are simply the *content* of the field. Seeing the difference between *context* and *content* is enormously empowering because when you see that the real you is not the *content*—you don't have to be run by it anymore.

Also seeing the difference between the observer and thoughts means you can shift your focus from identifying with *content* (thoughts) to identifying with *context* (the field of awareness/consciousness in which thoughts are arising). This shift in focus immediately re-contextualizes all events and experiences for you and as a result you are able to see things in the larger perspective. This is the key to understanding the compassion and light-heartedness you notice in wise people.

So what are you?

Once you make this important discovery—that you are not your thoughts but the observer of the thoughts that arise and disappear—the question naturally arises—*who then are you?* Or even better *what are you?*

This is the great existential question isn't it?

So what's the answer?

If you keep looking back at what is observing, you will discover what all the Great Ones throughout human history have discovered—that this *you* that is watching and observing is consciousness itself. As I said before, this is the most basic and fundamental quality of existence. Consciousness we find is the ground and pre-condition for everything we experience in life. Without consciousness, there is no experience.

If you are in doubt about this, ask yourself—are you conscious right now? And the answer is yes. Of course you are, otherwise how could you be reading this book? Consciousness is a prior (before) all human activity. It must be. So consciousness is a precondition to everything—to every experience. Consciousness is the background upon which everything unfolds and takes place. Consciousness is the field of awareness, the Ultimate Reality, the context in which all content (all thoughts, feelings, and sensations) arises and disappears.

Reality check: Who are you?

You can identify with consciousness itself—or with the content of consciousness (your thoughts). Identifying with consciousness itself is the direct route to the Ultimate Reality, the Self.

LAW 3: THE LAW OF NAMING

Thoughts name the world

As we move along in our study of the way the mind works, we come to the next law which describes how our minds interpret the world around us. Here's what happens.

When we look at the world, we think we see a "this" and a "that" and a "you" and a "me". But in reality, according to modern science, what we regard as the solid physical world is in fact one continuous, unbroken field of energy. According to Quantum Mechanics, these waves of energy become particles or localized space-time events that pop out of the field when there is an observer. Other traditions call this one field, the Absolute, the Ultimate Reality, Rigpa, the Tao, God, Brahman, and so forth (see box).

The non-dual field is reality and in this reality, everything is everything and there is no this or that... until...

Naming

Until we name the field.

Naming is the name of the game we play. Let's see what we do.

When we are born, we have no language. And then our parents teach us.

On the most basic level, we learn to simply name the world — that's how we all begin. Our mother and father teach us to say "tree", "house", "car", "girl", "boy", "man", "woman", "computer", "refrigerator", ice cream, and so forth. This is what the world teaches us.

This past year I have had the privilege of watching my son and his wife teach my little grandson Adam who is two and a half to name the world. It's fascinating to watch. And it makes me wonder—what was his experience of the world before his parents started teaching him to name things? (And what was our experience before our parents taught us to name things?) What did things look like then? Is this why my grandson bumped into things before he learned to name things? Was it because he didn't experience reality as separate things and people? But now he is learning to separate because his parents tell him, "This is a house. This is a car. You are a boy." It's fascinating to watch. Right now he's been calling himself, "the boy"! Fascinating, fascinating. Does that mean he is still regarding himself from the viewpoint of the greater consciousness (the observer) that we all are? I wonder!

But obviously, this naming of the world is a vitally important and very useful tool that allows us to navigate our way through life. And for most of us, it's a completely automatic and innocent process—we do it all the time without thinking about what we are doing. And even after we've grown up, we continue to do this every day of our life, starting every morning. Starting every morning when we wake up—we name the world with our thoughts. Yes, our thoughts name the world. If you watch yourself closely, you can see yourself doing this when you wake up in the morning.

If you don't understand what I mean, have your ever had the experience of waking up and not knowing who you were or where you were? And just for an instant feeling totally blank? And then you remembered, oh I'm so-and-so and I'm here in bed and that's my husband lying next to me and I've got to get up and go to work... and the whole world comes flooding back in (or so you think – and so it does!). Well that's what I mean, if you look carefully just as you wake up, you will see how you do this every single morning.

But to go back to the levels of naming. As I said, we learn to

name the world and the first level of naming is simple nouns—
"boy", "house", "car", "chair", "cat", "bread", and so forth.

But that's only the beginning.

On the next level of naming, we put nouns together into
sentences and thoughts become more descriptive. We say, "the
big house next door", "her new car is blue", "my computer is
working again", "the tree over there is so beautiful" and so forth.
And again, this is all very well and innocent enough. We name
the world and then start telling stories about it.

And then we start to believe our stories. We believe our stories
are reality and that this *is* the world.

Realty check: Quantum mechanics

Now we can see how we name the one field of reality that
is' before us. Quantum mechanics says this is what is
actually happening. Science has now proven that observation by a conscious observer is responsible for the
collapse of the wave function (Heisenberg principle). In
other words, the waves of energy or potential become
actual time-space events when they are observed.
Phenomenon pops out of the field when we focus our
attention on it.

Stories and judgments

But there's more.

On the next level, our stories become more complex and we
begin to make judgments. We start telling stories about good and
bad, right and wrong. We say "It's not good that he spends so
much time in front of the computer", "She shouldn't drive so fast,
it's reckless", "The people in the house next door should cut
down that tree because it's blocking the sun in my yard", and so

forth. We start making value judgments. We say things "should" or "shouldn't" be a certain way. We say things are "good" or "bad". And once we've named "this" or "that", we start comparing "this" and "that" to each other. Everything gets more and more complicated and we believe this *is* the world. But the question is, is this really the world? Is it?

Or is it just our stories?

What happened to the unbroken field of energy that is all of it? Where did it go? Well actually it didn't go anywhere, we just became so engrossed in—and identified with—our thoughts and stories that we lost sight of it—and eventually forgot all about it!

Non-dualism

Non-dualism refers to the Nature of Reality, the one field, the Absolute or Ultimate Reality in which there are no distinctions or dichotomies. The Nature of Reality is One and therefore all dualities are illusions—they are unreal and at best they are simply mental constructions we use for convenience.

Most of the world's greatest spiritual traditions are non-dual. Here are some of the basic concepts or terms you will encounter:

Advaita—from the Hindu tradition—literally means non-duality. Advaita refers to the identity of the Self (Atman) and the Whole (Brahman). Two of the great modern teachers in this tradition are the American psychiatrist David R. Hawkins and the Indian master Sri Nisargadatta Maharaj.

Brahman (from Hinduism) refers to the unchanging,

---

infinite, immanent and transcendent Reality.

Rigpa—from the Tibetan Dzogchen tradition—means our ultimate nature, the ground luminosity, the state of omniscience or enlightenment.

God—from the Christian tradition is also the Absolute and Infinite Reality. God is the one Divine Principle governing all existence.

Zen—a non-dual tradition from the East that seeks to realize the Absolute in all activities by means of experience. Awakening is to be achieved through meditation and the direct, experiential realization of the Nature of Reality.

Tao—a Chinese tradition. In the Tao Te Ching, the Tao or path is described as follows: "The Way that can be described is not the true Way. The Name that can be named is not the constant Name." The Tao is believed to be transcendent and without form and cannot be named or categorized. In other words, the Tao (the Nature of Reality) is basically indefinable. It has to be experienced.

Buddhism— There are many paths and types of Buddhism. The Buddha himself Siddhartha Gautama (commonly known as the Buddha or the Awakened One) is said to have experienced the Ultimate Reality and then spent the rest of his life trying to translate and teach what he experienced to others.

And now that we have looked at how we name the world and tell stories about it—let's look at what happens when we believe in the stories we are telling about the one field of reality that we are living in. What happens when we believe what we think?

Law 4: THE LAW OF CAUSE AND EFFECT

Thought is cause, experience is effect

Our thinking—the thoughts that we entertain—determine our experience of life. This is the great law of life on this plane. In brief, this means that our experience of reality (or this thing called life) is the result of our thoughts about life or reality—and not the result of experiencing reality itself directly.

And again, this is an impersonal, universal law. It has nothing to do with who you are or what you do. It doesn't matter how young or old you are or if you are rich or poor. This law applies to everyone—without exception—which is why it is a law.

This law means:

Whatever you think, you get to experience.

Whatever I think, I get to experience.

When you think something is great, you get to experience that. When you think something is terrible, you get to experience that.

Nothing else is going on.

Reality is what it is.

It's our interpretation we get to live. But again, don't believe me. Read on and then test this for yourself.

> We experience what we believe in,
> especially what we believe in with conviction.

Your first reaction to the above might be "Oh but this is not true.

Everyone can see that 'such-and-such' is a terrible thing. It has nothing to do with my thinking!" But you have to look more closely and ask yourself if this is really true. Because you will discover when you look closely, that everything under the sun is interpreted in a multitude of different ways by a multitude of different people. The exact same event is experienced in very different ways by different people. And this applies to our health, finances, relationships, you name it. What is excellent health for one person is a poor condition for the next. A lot of money to one person is almost not enough for the next. A big issue in one person's relationship doesn't matter at all to another. What seems politically correct to one person is completely wrong to another. And it's the same at the workplace. One person experiences working on a certain project with a tight deadline as highly stressful, while another thinks it's just an exciting challenge. One person hates working late and just wants to get home to the family while another person loves working late because he/she doesn't especially want to go home to the family!

So our experience is always entirely subjective—always—and always based on who we are and what we believe is good or bad for us. There is no neutral, objective definition of a "good" or "bad" event. It all depends on the point of view and the belief systems of the person (people) involved. And our points of view depend on a multitude of things including how we were programmed, our culture, our religion, our background, our sex, our age, and so on.

And even this changes for each individual as they mature and evolve because most people discover over time that what they once perceived and experienced as a "bad" event can turn out to be a "good" event when seen from another perspective. Hence the saying—*a blessing in disguise.*

So please consider this carefully and honestly. If you do, I can assure you that you will discover that all our reactions (yours and mine and everyone else's) in any and every situation are based on the thoughts and beliefs we have about life and our beliefs as to the meaning of these situations and events.

And so we find that in all situations, the basic mechanism is *thought is cause and experience is effect*. This is what is going on—at all times for everyone.

So take a look again and you will see that when something happens, if we think it's good, we feel good about it and we experience it as good. And when something happens and we think it's bad, we then feel bad about it and experience it as bad. And this has absolutely nothing whatsoever to do with the event itself. The event is just the event. And we discover that in truth, there is no connection whatsoever between an event and our reactions to it. The way we experience events is completely determined by our thoughts about the events.

Thought → experience...

So we discover that everything we experience is the effect of our thinking. And this is *the law of cause and effect* in action. Unfortunately, most people are unaware of this process because they don't know *the law of cause and effect*. And as a result, they don't see it happening. They don't see that an event takes place (something happens) and then they immediately click into their interpretations of the event. It happens so fast that most people don't notice the process. Instead they just think "oh this is bad" and put the so-called blame on the outside event. They don't see the middle step—the way in which our thinking, our interpretation of the event triggers our reaction and our experience.

But the fact is—reality is what it is and the rest is just thoughts in our minds. And our thoughts are not the direct experience itself, but only our interpretation of events. So it's our interpretation we get to live. We tell ourselves stories about events, people, and things and what they mean—and then we get to live it. This is our only experience.

* * *

If this is the first time you've met this concept, you will probably find it extremely challenging. And it is—because it's such a radical shift in perspective from everything we've learned and were taught to believe about life. But this doesn't make it any less true, so please observe and confirm this mechanism for yourself and find out if it's true. Because if it is, the consequences are truly amazing and liberating!

Reality check: So what happens if we drop our thoughts about the meaning of what's going on?

First of all is this possible? Can we drop our thoughts about what's going on? And if we can—even for just a few moments—what then do we experience?

Well let's give it a try.

Here's what to do. After you read this, put this book down and take a look at what is going on right now, right where you are. With no thoughts about the meaning of what's going on. Can you do this for just a minute or two? And when you do this, what do you experience?

When I try, the first thing I always notice (when I let go of my thoughts about the meaning of what's going on) is that it suddenly gets very peaceful and quiet. The second thing I notice is that there is only me, here and now. And that's about it. There is this moment with whatever is going on. And I'm just in it or I am just it! For example, this moment right now, just me sitting in front of my computer. Or it could be this moment walking down the street with the sun on my face. Or this moment, drinking a cup of tea. Or brushing my teeth. Or doing the dishes. Or talking to a friend.

That's about it.

Life is right before me.

Plain and simple.

And it's very peaceful.

Interesting isn't it?

To experience the present moment without any interpretations or thoughts about the meaning of what is going on is a very interesting experience. If you can find this space, try to rest there for a moment or two—without judging or forming any opinions about this moment. If you can do this for just a moment, I am quite sure *the law of cause and effect* will make perfect sense to you because you will see that without interpretations, there is just this moment. Without thinking about the past or the future, there is absolutely nothing to compare this moment to. There is only this moment—*this*—exactly as it is—happening now.

Usually we don't see this because we're so busy living our interpretation of what's going on. We are comparing "this" to "that". We think "this is good" or "that is bad" and then we get to experience "this is good" or "that is bad" instead of the pristine simplicity of this moment.

And well, this is the story of our lives—your life and of my life too. Your experience is your interpretation of what's going on. My experience is my interpretation of what's going on.

This is a pretty wild discovery isn't it? Why? Because when we understand *the law of cause and effect*, it means we have nothing to deal with but our own thoughts. Reality never gives us any problems—it's our thinking that does! And even though I have been saying this for years in all my books, the ramifications of this discovery are just mind-boggling and continue to be mind-boggling.

So now you know.

If you want to know the truth, there is only one place to look and that's inside yourself! Because *the law of cause and effect* tells us that all our experiences are internal events.

And that's life!

So the big question is—who decides what your experience of life is going to be like? Good question right?

This leads us to the next big discovery—that it is our identification with our thoughts that makes us suffer! Another mind-boggling discovery indeed!

Because what in fact makes us suffer?

What can possibly make us suffer?

Only our interpretation of an event can make us suffer.

Only our thoughts can make us suffer.

Nothing else is going on.

**Reality check: Arguing with reality
is the only suffering**

Reality is neither "good" nor "bad". Reality just is. But all thoughts and actions have consequences. This is the law of cause and effect.

Law 5: THE LAW OF EMOTION

You can't have an emotion without having a thought first

This important law says: *Thought precedes emotion.* Thought is always the cause of emotion. In other words, you can't have an emotion without having a thought first.

This comes as a surprise to many people because once they have heard about the law of cause and effect—*that thought is the cause and experience is effect*—they often ask "but what about emotions"? And they will say things like, "I wasn't thinking anything in particular, I just felt sad (or angry, upset, irritated, depressed, afraid... etc.)."

And the answer is that yes perhaps it *seems* as if these emotions just appeared, but the truth is a thought or a group of thoughts and beliefs always precede every emotion, whatever the emotion is. Because the impersonal and automatic mechanism is *you can't have an emotion without having a thought first.*

Thought comes first.

Thought ALWAYS precedes emotion.

Please consider this carefully and test it for yourself. When you do, you will discover that you cannot be angry without having an angry thought first. It is impossible. Even if you think you are not thinking a specific "angry" thought at the very moment you are feeling angry, you will find if you look closely that you have thoughts and beliefs about the situation, event or person which make you feel angry. If you did not—if you did not have the thought or belief that there is something about the situation or person that is wrong, inappropriate or incorrect in some way—you could simply not feel angry. It would be impossible. The same is true about feeling sad. You cannot be sad without having a sad thought first. It's just not possible, even if you can't consciously put your finger on the so-called specific sad thought, there must be something about the event, situation or person that corresponds to your beliefs about what is sad. The same holds true for feeling loving and kind. You can't feel loving and kind about anything or anyone without having loving and kind thoughts and attitudes first. Again, even if the specific "loving and kind" thought is not apparent, your basic belief system makes you react in this way. (See the Law of Underlying Beliefs on page 64 for more about this).

For most people, this realization is a true revelation—especially because so many people seem to be driven by their emotions. To recognize and understand how our thinking triggers our emotions—both in ourselves and in other people—is a major shift in consciousness and a sign that we are waking up to reality. It also means that we are starting to understand the way the mind works and influences our lives.

Understanding that thought precedes emotion also helps us understand the ways in which we are responsible for our own experiences, even though for most of us, the mechanism has been operating automatically and we were not conscious of what was going on. But now we are waking up and we are beginning to see how this law is operating in our lives. With this new under-standing, we can see that we are not victims of outside forces which are beyond our control, but rather that we experience and perhaps suffer from our own unconscious beliefs and programming. This gives us the option of examining our thoughts and choosing to react more wisely in the future.

Reality Check: The mind-emotion-body connection

Let's try experimenting with the mind-emotion-body connection.

To experience this connection, I suggest you sit quietly by yourself for a few moments and try the following. It will only take a minute or two. Begin by closing your eyes and breathing deeply.

- *The Lemon*: Start by envisioning that you are eating a lemon. What happens when you do this? Just the thought of putting a sour lemon into your mouth immediately triggers a physical reaction in your body. Your mouth contracts and you start to salivate. All this happens despite the fact that there is no actual physical lemon. Just the thought of a lemon is enough to trigger a concrete physical reaction in your body.

- *The Scoundrel*: Now take this exercise one step further and think of someone you feel has wronged you terribly. Rehearse for a moment all the wrongs you feel this person has committed against you. What emotions do you feel? What physical symptoms do these thoughts trigger? Increased heart beat? A feeling of heat? Anger? Hatred? Rage? A feeling of tension? A feeling that your whole body is contracting? Observe yourself—your emotions and your body—as you entertain these thoughts.

- *The Angel*: Now think of someone who you know loves you dearly. Someone who has always understood you and supported you. Someone who truly sees all your good sides. What do you feel now? What emotions do these thoughts trigger? And what physical symptoms do these emotions trigger? Do you suddenly feel much calmer? Do you experience a feeling of expansion in your chest—and release in your whole body? Do you feel comfortable, happy and relaxed?

Now you can see that just by entertaining three very different thoughts, you were able to trigger and experience three very different emotional and physical states in yourself. Continue to observe your own and other people's behavior until you understand the true relationship between your thoughts and your emotions and physical sensations.

Order of phenomena

The order in which phenomena occur is always—thoughts first—then the emotional reaction—and then the physical reaction. This is true even though it is usually happening so fast that we don't perceive it.

This is very interesting to contemplate because when we realize that thought is the causative factor behind emotions, we also have an important clue in healing disease. Today much research has been done into the mind-body connection which clearly demonstrates the multitude of ways our thinking is affecting our health. And scientists have now proven that every thought we think creates or triggers a biochemical reaction in our bodies. This is a revolution in our view of the way our bodies work—and why we get sick. With this knowledge, we can contemplate and better understand the deep, long-term value of positive thoughts and intentions because now we know they will create positive emotions which will result in positive changes in our physical bodies as well. Unfortunately, because most people are unaware of this mechanism, many of us are doing the exact opposite—they are dwelling on negative thoughts which trigger negative emotions which in turn create stress in our bodies.

But please don't misunderstand me here. I'm not saying it's your fault if you get sick! That's simply too simplistic a view of what's going on. Obviously no one does that. Rather I am simply pointing out that our new understanding of the mind-body connection tells us that when a person's underlying beliefs and basic thought patterns and attitudes are negative and disharmonious, this can result in emotional distress and perhaps later manifest as physical symptoms and illness.

This also means that armed with this new understanding, we can examine our own thinking patterns and programming and perhaps better understand the ways in which we are creating stress, unhappiness, emotional imbalance and perhaps even physical imbalances in our lives. And we can also understand why it is so important to learn how to identify, investigate, and release our negative emotions, thoughts and beliefs—and replace them with a more positive approach to life. Quite simply because it's good for our emotional and physical health! Yes, peace of mind is good for our health! (For more about investigating negative thoughts and beliefs, see the section on Investigation tools on page 132).

The one real emotion: Unconditional love

There is, however, one real emotion that has nothing to do with our thinking—and that's unconditional love. Unconditional love is our true nature and therefore precedes thought. But this type of love—unconditional love—is not what most people mean by love. Most people, when they talk or think about love, mean conditional love—the kind of love that says "if you do what I want you to do, I'll love you". That's the most common kind of love we see. (And I'm not even sure this really is love.) But anyway, most people say they love each other as long as they agree with each other and then when they disagree, they get divorced! Parents seem to love their kids as long as they go to school and behave themselves, but when they drop out and start smoking dope, their parents often don't. So obviously, this type of love is conditional—it depends on the other person's behavior. And it depends on our thoughts and beliefs about what is good and bad, right and wrong, etc. So it is conditional. It depends on a whole host of factors.

And this (conditional love) has nothing to do with our true nature, which is the vast awareness (or consciousness), the Ultimate Reality, the Truth of Being that we are. And the Truth of Being, the Ultimate Reality *is unconditional love.* Now why do I say that? Well, first all of because the Ultimate Reality is unconditional support. The Ultimate Reality is supporting all of us and all of life without conditions. It just does. Obviously It does or none of us would be here. This One Ultimate Reality — whatever It is — has given us the gift of life (for no reason whatsoever). In other words, this One Life created us and now sustains and maintains us regardless of who or what we are, regardless of what we think, and regardless of how we use this precious gift of life that we've all been given. This One Life, this Ultimate Reality, just supports us. It's like the sun which shines equally on all...

Law 6: THE LAW OF FOCUS

What you focus your attention on grows

This law teaches us that *whatever we focus our attention on grows.*

This is a far-reaching and very empowering discovery. It means we energize whatever we focus our attention on. Our attention "brings to life" out of the vast field of infinite energy or pure potentiality whatever we focus on. This has now been confirmed by Quantum mechanics which has proven that observation by a conscious observer is responsible for the collapse of the wave function (Heisenberg principle) into actual particles in the field of potentiality. In other words, the waves of energy or potential that make up the field of reality that we live and move and breathe in become actual time-space events when they are observed. This is how phenomenon pops out of the field when we focus our attention on it.

The power of attention

Attention, it seems, is the magic wand of creation—at least when it comes to your experiences and mine! So let me ask you—how are you using your power of attention? How are you using this, amazing ability, this priceless gift?

Are you focusing on difficulties, lack, and illness or are you focusing on all the blessings in your life right now? What exactly are you doing? If you want to live a happy live, it's important to take the time to take a good look at exactly what you are doing. Ask yourself—what is the general tone of your thinking? Is it a praiseful song of gratitude from morning to evening for the blessings of life—or is it one long complaint? And what is your experience? If you look carefully (and are honest) you will see that your experience is a perfect reflection of your focus. Always! And again this is because *thought is cause and experience is effect.* So when we look at the power of our thinking in terms of what we focus on, we see it is all about learning to use the power of our attention wisely. This is an extremely important key when it comes to understanding why our lives are like they are. And it's also extremely empowering because we can learn to consciously direct the power of our focus.

So let's look more closely at this phenomenon.

Focusing on this moment

Here's a big one. What is the general drift or tendency of your mental life? Do you spend a lot of time dwelling on the past? Or are you one of those people who is always worrying about the future? And does the thought of the future give you anxiety and sleepless nights? So much so that you fail to actually notice this moment?

Or do you actually notice this moment? Are you mindful enough to actually be able to focus enough on what is happening right now? Are you able to actually experience and enjoy this moment? It's embarrassing but the honest truth is that most of us have a pretty hard time doing this. Most of us spend most of our lives somewhere else (at least in thought)!

And frankly, you might not even be conscious of what you are doing. And if you're not conscious of what you are doing, you might not be aware of the fact that you actually have a choice! You might not realize that you can actually choose what you focus your attention on. But of course to do this, you must first notice what you're actually doing. So you have to start by watching yourself for a while so you become aware of the general drift or tendency of your daily thinking. Once you become aware of this, you can begin to exercise the power of choice and begin to consciously choose what you focus your attention on.

And yes, it sounds simple, but it's not always easy to do—especially in the beginning. And no, there's isn't any magic wand or secret formula that makes this happen all at once and forever. Rather learning to focus the power of your attention is a lifelong project.

But don't despair! Just the fact that you are becoming aware of your thoughts and how you are using the power of focus is a great step forward. Especially if you can see that you are using the power of your attention in a negative way. This awareness means you are beginning to understand the way the mind works and that you are more and more able to see the cause and effect relationship between your thoughts and your experiences. This is crucial if you want to become the master of your focus.

It's also important to realize that choosing our focus is our only freedom. This is where we exercise our free will. (See the next law—The Law of Free Will—for details). So keep noticing what you are doing and keep practicing. Make up your mind to focus on the Highest and Best you can conceive of. And do it again. And again! This is the magic and joy of life. This is the great adventure. So enjoy your adventure and enjoy learning. Amazing things will happen as you become better and better at focusing on the wonder of this moment!

Reality check: Use the gift of attention wisely

If you focus on lack, you will experience lack.
If you focus on the abundance of your life, you will experience abundance.
If you focus on love, you will experience love.

Focus and health

What is your focus when it comes to your health? This is a very interesting and challenging question for most of us. When you're not feeling well, do you focus on every ache and pain—or do you focus on the wonderful strength and healing power of your body and of Life itself? You can see this is a most important question and crucial choice, especially when we know that whatever we focus our attention on grows.

According to the law of focus, if we feel weak and then focus our attention on feeling weak, we will feel even weaker. Because whatever we focus our attention on grows. And if that is the case, then the reverse must also be true. If we focus on strength—on whatever strength we do have—we will feel stronger. Which means we have an amazing power at our disposal in terms of health and healing—so why not use it?

When you think about it, it's quite fascinating to realize that we have this amazing power at our disposal and we're not using it! How can it be that we're not using this priceless gift? Obviously because most of us don't know about the power of focus! We don't know it exists because nobody taught us how the mind works. So we don't recognize this power or understand what it is and how to use it. Instead we are walking around in a daze, asleep to our true power.

But now you are waking up! So claim your true power and think about the law of focus when you're feeling ill. And use this wonderful power wisely. Watch yourself carefully and see what you are thinking and saying and focusing your attention on. And if you discover that you are sabotaging yourself and your recovery, you can start changing your focus now! It's never too late.

Here's a wonderful affirmation by Florence Shovel Shinn that can help you get on the right track when it comes to your health: *"I praise what strength I have. I give thanks for what health I have. I glory in what life I have and God now gives the increase."* (See the section on Focus tools on page 97 for more about how to use the power of focus wisely).

> Thinking positive is closer to the truth.

Focus and challenges

The same holds true for all the many challenges and so-called problems we face in our daily lives. What is the focus of our attention when we face so-called difficulties? Do we focus on the potential in each situation and how everything in life is supporting us or do we focus on the hassle, the inconvenience, and the irritation? When you know about the power of focus, you can see how important your choice is.

So make up your mind that whatever it is, you are going to grow stronger because of it and evolve into a more magnanimous and compassionate person—and watch yourself turn every situation into a true blessing, for yourself and everyone involved!

Context or content?

Another good way of looking at the power of focus is to consider whether you are putting your attention on the larger context (the big perspective) which you can say is the unfolding of this mysterious thing we call life—or if you are focusing on the content, which are your thoughts and emotions concerning every particular little event and situation you meet along your way.

When you realize that there is a difference between the observer (you) and your thoughts, (see Law 2: The Law of Witnessing on page 26) it becomes easier to shift your focus away from the content (which is your thoughts) to the context (which is the vast field of beingness or awareness/consciousness in which all thoughts are arising and which is you). When you shift your focus from content to context, it automatically re-contextualizes the thoughts and experiences you are having at the present moment and puts them into the larger perspective. And with your focus on the big view, you realize that you cannot see the end of all things. You also see that you don't honestly know what is good or bad! (Good or bad again being just relative value judgments or positions which depend on our perspective at a particular moment in time. See box below.) When you see things like this you instantly become more light-hearted and can allow life to unfold with effortless ease!

Reality check: Who knows what is good or bad?

We often think of good and bad, hot and cold, light and dark, right and wrong as opposites. But is this true? Is there an absolute, objective standard of good/bad, hot/cold, light/dark, right/wrong? If we look closely we discover that all dualities are in fact just mental constructions. They are relative concepts—they are all just positions in an infinite range of possible positions.

Let's look at a few examples.

Hot and cold: It's 0C degrees here in Copenhagen right now. Is this hot or cold? Well, compared to the temperature in Johannesburg, South Africa where my friend lives, yes it's very cold because the temperature in Johannesburg is +25C right now. But compared to the temperature in Wisconsin where my grandson is at the moment, it is actually warm here in Copenhagen because the temperature in Wisconsin is almost –20C.

Light and dark: It's afternoon and it's a grey, foggy winter day here in Copenhagen. If I compare this to a summer day when the sun is shining brightly, it's actually pretty dark here in Copenhagen right now. But again if I compare this grey, foggy afternoon to the dead of night

---

when there is no moon, well it's actually pretty bright outside right now. So it's really a matter of more or less light.

Good and bad: I have a migraine headache and feel pretty lousy. Compared to a day when I am feeling energetic and full of piss and vinegar, this headache seems bad. But if I compare my condition to the condition of my ex-husband who just died of terminal liver cancer, my physical condition is actually very good, even with a migraine headache!

Right and wrong: Most of us believe in "right" and "wrong". For example, it's "wrong" to lie. But is it always wrong to lie? Yes you say. OK, well let's say it's the Second World War and you are hiding a family of Jews in your cellar. One day the Gestapo knocks on your door and asks you if you are hiding Jews in your cellar. If you believe it's wrong to lie, will you say, "Yes I am." Or will you lie to save the lives of these people?

And what about our belief that killing someone is "wrong"? What happens if someone is trying to kill your child? Would you kill that person to protect your child and save her life? And would your action be "wrong"? This of course is what we call situational ethics — and courts of law are always faced with this type of question. Judges and juries must take into consideration the situation and motive of a person's behavior before passing judgment on what is "right" or "wrong".

The more we consider dualities, the more we can see that there is only one reality and that dualities are relative positions in the larger context.

It's your choice

So we see that what we focus our attention on grows. You focus your attention on something/someone/some thought and then you get to experience what you focused on. For more about how to use the power of focus more wisely in your life, see the many focus tools described in detail in the section about focus tools beginning on page 97.

It is also important to remember that the focus of our attention is always our choice—*always!* We are the choice-makers—always—whether we are conscious of what we are choosing/doing or not. And this leads us to the next law.

Law 7: THE LAW OF FREE WILL

You *can* choose

You are the only thinker in your mind. This is the most wonderful discovery anyone can ever make. It is the key to freedom — the high road. Because when you understand this, you also understand that you *can* become the conscious choice-maker in your life and choose. You *can* become the one who decides.

Most people today are asleep — unaware that they have the ability to choose the focus of their attention. But just because a person is unaware and does not consciously exercise his or her ability to choose the focus of his/her attention, the reality is that in every moment *there is a choice*.

This ability to choose the focus of our attention is our greatest gift. It is the gift of free will. This ability to choose our focus is what makes us free individuals. If this was not the case — if we could not think for ourselves and choose our focus, we would not be free. But we can, because no one else can get into another person's mind and think for them. Please think deeply about it — and you will see how truly amazing this is. Yes it is true that most people are as yet unaware of this fact — and are just following their old unconscious programming without questioning it. And yes it is true that most people are not yet consciously using this power, but the power is there nevertheless.

But you say what about when people are forced to do things against their will? And yes it is also true that people can use force on the outer plane to coerce other people to do or say things, but no one can get into another person's mind and think for them. This is where we are always free. Each person is always free in their own mind. Each person is always the only thinker in their mind.

This is what makes us human beings.

This is what makes human life so precious, because we have the ability to be aware of what we are thinking and we have the ability to choose the focus of our attention—this is something we *can* do. This is what makes us free.

Having free will is our greatest gift and privilege. It is also our greatest challenge!

Why? Because no matter what is happening around you—*no matter what*—no matter what anyone says or does, you and you alone (whether you are aware of what you are doing or not) choose the focus of your attention. No one else can make this choice for you. Only you can do it.

That is why we are the choice-makers.

This choice is our only freedom.

Free will is our only freedom.

And whether we are aware of it or not, we are always exercising this privilege, this freedom because we are always choosing.

So please wake up to the fact that you are choosing right now—and every single minute of every single day (whether you are aware of it or not).

Nothing else is going on.

And nothing is more important—or more wonderful than this!

So contemplate this until you fully understand the significance (and power) of free will. Free will is what we are. Free will is our true nature, our essence. Free will is all we have, and fortunately for us, free will is everything!

When you observe what you are doing with this in mind, you will see that this is true. In every now moment (even if you are not aware of what you are doing) you are choosing the focus of your attention. You are either focusing on this or on that. In every situation, you are making a choice. Either you are focusing on the potential and the goodness of the situation or person before you or you are choosing to focus on the limitations and the negative in the situation or person before you. And it's always like this. From the very smallest, most insignificant events in our lives like standing in line at the supermarket to the so-called big and important events in our personal relationships, careers and on the world stage.

When we understand this, we will also understand why the Wise say it's all about *you* — and it's always all about *you*. Nothing else is going on but your choice of focus.

> You choose your focus
> and then you get to experience your choice.
> It's as simple as that.

Learning to choose wisely

This is why it is so important to learn to choose wisely!

Because we get to experience all our choices!

So it makes sense to learn to focus our attention wisely. This is what all the great teachers have been telling us throughout the ages — the importance of exercising your free will and choosing wisely.

Learning to choose wisely requires self-discipline. Learning to choose wisely means following your wisdom rather than choosing immediate pleasure. The Wise tell us that even if this is difficult, it is necessary if we wish to evolve on the pathway of life and achieve our highest potential.

Obviously this is no news to any thinking person because everyone knows that success in any field requires self-discipline. Successful people make up their minds, focus on their goals, and are disciplined about reaching them. Just think about the people you admire. How did they become great? The great leaders, the great athletes, the great musicians, the great artists, the great spiritual teachers—how did they achieve what they achieved? They used their free will to choose a course of action and then they focused all their attention on their goals. They used their free will to spend time learning and practicing their skills!

And what about successful business people? No one is successful in the world of business without exercising a great deal of self-discipline. The same goes for politicians, world leaders, and for good parents, good teachers and good partners. Everyone who succeeds at achieving anything learns to use their free will wisely and to exercise self-discipline.

The same goes for happiness! Even though people may think happiness is a haphazard event, true happiness isn't haphazard. Achieving true happiness requires self-discipline too! Now I am not talking about random or accidental type of happiness that comes from outer events and which depends on other people and circumstances. I am talking about true happiness, the deep inner happiness which is our natural state and which arises in wise people who are living in harmony with this thing calls life. The people who experience this deep inner happiness see the Nature of Reality and understand the way the mind works. This kind of happiness is stable and comes from within. It is unconditional because it does not depend on outer circumstances.

For those of us on the path who can see and understand this, realizing this inner state and achieving this kind of happiness requires continual self-discipline. Achieving this goal requires constant study and daily contemplation of this thing called life. Plus using our free will to practice the techniques and focus required to cultivate and nourish this deep inner peace and inner happiness. This is what spiritual practice is all about. And of course what most self-help books and books about personal development and spiritual growth are about. The best books describe practices for self-empowerment and spiritual growth which require study, daily practice and self-discipline.

> Most people work with their bodies,
> but not with their minds.

Daily practice and self-discipline

Here are some examples of the types of practices I am talking —
all of which require active use of our free will. The practices
described below may seem simple, but anyone who has ever tried
any of them knows they require making a conscious choice and
then exercising a great deal of self-discipline!

Practicing non-judgment: A good focal point on the spiritual
pathway is making the decision to let go of our judgments about
people, things and events. This is an excellent practice because
we use so much mental energy judging people, things and events
all the time and this creates a great deal of inner turbulence.
Practicing non-judgment (in other words just letting things
unfold without engaging in an inner dialogue about them) quiets
the mind and slowly allows a deep inner stillness to emerge. But
practicing non-judgment, even for an hour a day, requires self-
discipline. To do this, you must use your free will. You must
decide to do this and keep practicing! Day in and day out!

Practicing non-resistance: Another good focal point is to use
your free will to decide not to resist whatever is happening in this
moment. Even though we may be unaware of it, many of us are
often at war with this moment. We are resisting what is
happening in our lives right now — and this creates a great deal of
stress and anxiety. So what happens when we stop resisting what
is happening right now? It's an amazing experience and
wonderful spiritual practice. But again, we are so used to

resisting what is, that it requires real focus and self-discipline to stop resisting this moment. Make a conscious choice and do this on a regular basis and see how it transforms your life! (See page 97 for more about this practice).

Practicing seeing the potential for good in every situation: Here's another good inner practice that requires active use of your free will. Making the choice to see the potential for good in every situation no matter what is going on—to see the highest and best in every person present. To do this requires constant awareness and control of your focus. You have to be aware of what you are thinking, doing and saying in order to do this. You must be mindful and self-conscious enough so when you find yourself dwelling on the negative, you are awake enough to realize that it's time to shift your focus. Again this requires constant vigilance which is why it is a demanding spiritual practice, unless of course you are Forrest Gump! (See the Law of Substitution on page 73 for more about this practice).

Practicing no gossip: Here's a wonderful practice I learned at Findhorn, a spiritual community in northern Scotland. This is what they attempt to do. Whenever a member of the community has something to say about another person, instead of talking behind the person's back, the community member must go up to that person and tell the person directly to his or her face what's it is her or she wants to say. In practice, this means that when you are talking to anyone in the community—if you have something to say about another person—they will tell you to go and tell it to that person instead of to them! This is a wonderful practice that requires a great deal of self-discipline! Try this for a few days and find out what a gossip you really are!

This was just a few examples of spiritual practices that require conscious choice and self-discipline. Obviously, there are so many excellent practices we can devote ourselves to such as:

Practicing mindfulness (being present in this moment)
Practicing compassion
Practicing forgiveness
Practicing service
Practicing meditation
Practicing silence for an hour a day

(See the section about focus tools on page 97 for detailed descriptions of some of these practices.)

The importance of intention

The Great Ones also tell us that intention is everything. Since it is difficult to see the end of all things or to know what is good or bad in the long term for ourselves or for anyone else, the motivation behind our actions should be our guiding light. What is the reason or motive for what you are doing? Is your intention love, kindness and compassion? Do you hope to ease the suffering of your fellow beings with your words and actions? Is your intention to be of service and help people? Or are you only thinking of short-term pleasure, material gain, and what's in it for you? According to the Wise, it is our motivation and intention which determines the karmic consequences of our thoughts and actions. Thus we see the importance of using our free will wisely and the importance of our intention when it comes to making wise choices.

So practice using the information you already have! Follow the wisdom you already have (which is always a lot more than we realize)! Remember what the Great Ones say.

Don't waste your precious time.

Follow your wisdom and not your emotions.

Exercise self-discipline.

Keep practicing and persevere.

Wake up to your true power and choose wisely!
Understanding this can and will change your life!

Reality check: It's your choice

Everything in this book is designed to help you slow down
and become more aware of your mental processes and of
what you are doing. As we learn to watch our minds and
our inner processes, we begin to see the mechanisms that
are running our lives. In this connection, as we learn to
watch our thoughts arising and disappearing again, we
discover that we also have a choice when it comes to
attaching to a thought or not. In other words, we start to
see that we don't actually have to believe all our thoughts!
We can, for example, just watch them arise and disappear
again. And we can question their validity. We can watch a
thought arising and ask ourselves—is this thought true?
Do I want believe this thought? Do I need to believe this
thought? Do I want to let my life be run by this thought or
belief? This ability to detach from our thoughts and
question them is also the power of the choice-maker. (For
more about how to question your thoughts see the section
about Investigation tools on page 132).

Law 8: THE LAW OF UNDERLYING BELIEFS

Your underlying beliefs determine your experience

Reality is what it is. Life is what it is. But our experience of this thing called life is determined by our thoughts and underlying beliefs about life—whether or not we are conscious of these thoughts and beliefs. And whether or not we are conscious of this mechanism.

And since our basic beliefs about life determine our experience of reality to a far greater degree than most of us realize, it will serve us well to investigate this phenomenon.

Now by underlying beliefs I do not mean our passing fancies, emotions or whims, or our changing, daily ideas and opinions about this and that. No, I mean our most basic underlying view or understanding of "Life". These are the ideas and beliefs that underlie everything we think, say and do. You could also say these are our most basic ideas and beliefs about what life is and the Nature of Reality.

These basic, underlying beliefs are something we learn from early childhood from our parents, society, teachers, the media, our religion and culture. You could say that from the moment we are born, we are programmed by the society we are born into— we learn the belief systems of our family and culture. And we are usually quite unaware or unconscious of the fact that we are being programmed. But this is what happens. We are all innocent children who simply believe what our parents and teachers tell us. Nor do we have a say about the way we are being programmed. This is just the way it is.

No independent individual views

Oh but you say, I'm an intelligent, independent individual with my own independent views on life and reality. And yes, you can say this is true to a certain extent. To a certain extent, each person has his or her own unique spin or version of the Nature of Reality, depending on his personal background, family, education, etc. which does result in different reactions to events and different life experiences, but this is not the whole story. Every individual is also to a greater or lesser extent influenced by their early programming which we usually call our cultural background or heritage.

Here's an example of what I mean. I was born in the US and lived there until I was 20. After traveling the world for some years, I ended up in Denmark where I have been living ever since. Once I settled here in Denmark, I discovered that the Danes have a unique, underlying belief they call the "Jante Law" and this "Jante Law" says *"Don't think you're anyone special or that you're better than us."* By this, the Danes mean that you shouldn't put yourself forward, be pushy—and worse yet—be boastful about your achievements.

I remember when I first heard this I thought it was a pretty strange law—and it didn't sound very serious or important to me. But slowly over the years, I began to see how this Jante Law influenced almost everything and everyone who lives here in Denmark and also in the other Nordic countries (the Swedes and Norwegians have this belief too). As a result of this cultural code, I started to realize how much it is frowned upon here in Scandinavia to appear to elevate oneself above one's peers or to claim to be better or smarter than others. This was of course very surprising to me because I grew up in America where we were taught that we should be proud of showing off our achievements.

Understanding the difference between the programming in Scandinavia and the US, made me understand why Danes, for example, consider Americans boastful and bragging when they talk about their achievements. Talking about your achievements is definitely considered a "no, no" in Scandinavia thanks to the Jante Law! In Denmark and Scandinavia (unlike America), modesty rules!

Underlying belief systems

Besides our underlying social and religious programming, we also pick up various life views from our family and the people we hang out with. Here are some more examples of various types of underlying belief systems that people have without usually being aware of them (and most people of course have a combination of several of the types described below):

The Materialist: People with this type of underlying belief system have a materialistic view of the Nature of Reality. They see the world as a purely material or physical phenomenon. "Life" or reality is what they can perceive with their physical senses and nothing more. There is no underlying cause behind this version of reality—life just appeared out of nowhere. Thus there is no order or reason for anything to happen. To people with this view, human life is the same as the life of an insect. There is no rhyme or reason for anything to happen and they often feel that life is totally haphazard. To them, all of life and all experience is just a matter of luck. Some people get squashed for no good reason while others are lucky and live long, happy lives. Who the lucky ones are is completely beyond their control.

The Sufferer: People with this view of "Life" focus their attention on the dualistic nature of experience. Everywhere they look, they see good and evil, darkness and light, love and hate, sickness and health, poverty and wealth, etc. In this view, there is much suffering in life as human beings swing back and forth between the pairs of opposites from which there is no escape. Often people with this view of the Nature of Reality believe that God has orchestrated this scenario. Some even believe that the difficulties they experience are punishment for sins they have committed.

The Fetish Worshipper: This is another spin on the materialistic/dualistic views of "Life" described above. People with this type of basic belief system believe their fate or destiny depends on outside forces, i.e., forces beyond their own control. These forces include concepts or ideas such as heredity, their horoscope (the position of the stars and planets), their sex, their age, their nationality, or their education. Often people with this view then decide to look to other outside forces in an attempt to create balance and harmony in their lives. Thus fetish worshippers give away their power to a wide variety of forces such as other people and/or external objects or phenomena (which is why I call them fetish worshippers). These outside forces or people could be a doctor, a teacher, the leader of a sect, the position of the planets, crystals and stones, essential oils, pills, the choice of colors, the arrangement of houses and furniture (feng shui), a healer, a psychiatrist, a special diet, medical treatment, alternative treatments, etc. In other words, a fetish worshipper is a person who gives the responsibility for his or her destiny to any outside force, person, regimen, thing or arrangement.

The Mountain Climber: People with this view of "Life" or underlying belief system are basically success-oriented. Whether their orientation tends to be more materialistic or spiritual, they basically believe in their own personal power, worth and ability to succeed. This underlying belief tends to support the view that "Life" is good and that human beings have the ability to create a good life for themselves and their families. This type of belief is usually at least some part of the belief pattern of most successful people in the world of business, sports, the arts and government.

The Believer: People with this view of "Life" usually believe there is some kind of order or meaning to "Life". Often they believe in God or some kind of higher power, which tends to include the assumption that human beings are part of an orderly evolution towards something higher and better. Many believers may believe in reincarnation as the Buddhists and Hindus do, which obviously changes one's whole perspective on this present life. In general, the belief in a higher power is an underlying belief system that influences every aspect of a person's life and circumstances, including the way the person meets the great transition called death.

Universal beliefs

There is an even more basic level of beliefs that are universal. These are the beliefs that are shared by almost everyone. These beliefs seem to be common to the human condition because almost everyone has these beliefs, regardless of their background, culture, religion, age, sex and status.

Again, these are underlying beliefs which we are often unaware of and which have a much greater influence on our choices, actions and experience of life than most of us realize. And unfortunately, these beliefs can wreck havoc on our lives—until we begin to be aware of them and learn to question their validity. (See the section on Investigation tools on page 132 for more about how to question these negative universal beliefs.)

Here are some examples of the universal beliefs that almost everyone has:

Life is dangerous.
Death is dangerous.
There is something wrong with me.
I'm not good enough.
Parents should love their children.
My mother should understand me.
Children should love their parents.
There shouldn't be war in the world.
I need his/her love to be OK.
I need more money.

It's his/her fault.
It's my fault.
I don't belong.
We need to save the world.
There is evil in the world.
My happiness depends on… (someone else or on something else)
I need a partner to be happy.
I did it wrong.

The above are just a few examples of the kind of thoughts or beliefs most people have to a greater or lesser degree.

So how do these universal beliefs affect us?

Let's take an example. Say for example you believe "life is dangerous"… This is one of the universal beliefs most people have (to a greater or lesser degree). You can try to watch yourself and see how many of your choices and how much of your behavior is governed by this belief. Think of all the situations where you would act differently if you didn't believe that "life is dangerous". Think of all the choices you make that reflect this belief. Think of all the precautions you take and all the things you don't dare to do… because you believe "life is dangerous".

So what will happen if you pick up this belief, hold it in your hands, and look it straight in the eye and question it! Who knows what you might find!

Let's give it a try and start with a belief that is closely connected to the belief that "life is dangerous" — it's the belief that "death is dangerous".

Is death dangerous?

The belief that "death is dangerous" is an idea that haunts many of us. So let's consider it. Is death really dangerous? If the answer to this question is yes, where's the proof? Is there any proof that death is dangerous?

The fact that people die, the fact that everyone dies, doesn't actually prove that death is dangerous, does it? All it proves is that death happens. But we don't really know if dying is dangerous at all do we? Because no one has ever come back from the dead and told us, have they? So where's the proof that death is dangerous?

In reality, there's no proof at all. No concrete evidence that death is dangerous. All we can say for sure is that death happens and the rest we don't know. That's reality. That's all we know. So what are we afraid of?

We're afraid of the idea, the thought "death is dangerous". Which leads us back to the thought we started with—the thought that "life is dangerous". It seems to me that these two thoughts are connected because it's pretty hard to believe in one of them without believing in the other! So let's look at "life is dangerous". Do we know if this thought is true? Because if we can't know for sure that death is dangerous, how can we know for sure that life is dangerous? You see how they go together? Because if you are afraid of death, you're probably afraid of life because you think something might happen to you and you could die! But if death isn't dangerous, how can life be dangerous?

It's fun and interesting to play around with thoughts like this and do it slowly as a kind of meditation and see what comes up. Not only do we begin to see how our minds work when we play around like this, but we can also see how we often terrify ourselves with underlying beliefs like this. Because we are unconscious of what we are doing, we make ourselves miserable without even knowing for sure if what we fear is true. This is the power of unquestioned underlying beliefs!

Slowing down the wheels of mind

This is also why learning to slow down the wheels of mind can be so enlightening. Finally, as we slow down, we get a chance to see what we are believing and how these beliefs are affecting our lives. It can be a pretty shocking experience, but also very liberating because this insight allows us to take back our power as the choice-makers in our lives and make better choices instead of being slaves to beliefs that we never questioned. (See the section on Investigation tools on page 132 for more about how to question our beliefs).

Reality check: Things just happen

The truth is things just happen. Our experience of events is a result of our beliefs and our interpretation of whether these happenings are good or bad, happy or sad, right or wrong, etc. That is all we are experiencing. Nothing else is going on. (Nothing else can go on.)

This is also why everyone, every single person, is living in his or her own world. At first this might sound strange to you; but once you have digested and understood the ideas in this book, you will understand why this is so. Each one of us lives in our own mental universe.

Collective belief patterns

The law of underlying beliefs also obviously applies to the mindsets of groups and to the collective consciousness of humanity as a whole. By groups I mean family units, tribes, racial and religious groups, regions, states and nations. Groups share certain underlying beliefs or collective stories. In fact, this is what makes them a group! Their common beliefs bring them together and keep them together. Since they share the same underlying beliefs and stories, they exhibit similar behavior patterns and share similar "Life" experiences.

Wars arise when whole groups share similar negative under-lying beliefs and stories about other groups such as "My group (family, tribe, religion, country) is better, superior to your group (family, tribe, religion, country)."

Uninvestigated collective beliefs often rule our behavior.

Law 9: THE LAW OF SUBSTITUTION

Change your thinking, change your life

Now that we know that we get to experience whatever we think—especially what we think with conviction—you might be reacting to all this by saying to yourself "yikes, but my thinking is so negative!" I know that is how I reacted when I realized that I could only experience my own thinking and that a lot of my thinking was pretty negative. It was rather terrifying, to say the least.

And then I thought, well I must stop thinking so negatively and think positively! But that (I quickly found out) is easier said than done. The mind doesn't work like that. You can't say to yourself, I am not going to think about something, because, well, when you say that to yourself you are actually thinking about whatever it is you don't want to think about! It's like me saying to you right now, "Don't think about the Statue of Liberty in the New York harbor." The moment I say that, what are you thinking about? The Statue of Liberty of course. That's just the way our minds work. But if I say to you, think about chocolate ice cream, what are you thinking about now? Chocolate ice cream, right and not the Statue of Liberty! Your attention shifted didn't it?

And this is what the great law of substitution is all about. It's based on the simple observation that you can't tell yourself to stop thinking about something. Because when you do, you are actually focusing your attention on whatever it is you don't want to think about. And that means even if it's something you don't want to think about—according to the law of focus—you are actually energizing the very thing you don't want to think about by telling yourself to stop thinking about it!

So what can we do about this?

How can we stop thinking negatively?

We can use the great law of substitution. This law tells us *you can only change your thinking by replacing old thoughts and thought patterns with new ones. In other words, by substituting new thoughts for the old ones.*

Mind moves in familiar patterns

This is important to know because we have to keep in mind the fact that our minds have a tendency to move in familiar patterns. If you begin observing the way you think and your thought patterns, you will discover that once your mind starts moving in a certain direction, it just seems to continue in that direction (unless something else pops up and gets your attention). The other thing you will notice is that we all have a tendency to keep thinking the same thoughts over and over again—like broken records. In fact if you watch, you will probably discover that 99% of what you are thinking today is a repetition of what you were thinking yesterday! Yes it's true. But don't believe me—try observing your thoughts for a whole day yourself. How many *completely new thoughts* did you actually think today? Were there any in fact? Which means, of course that if you are used to thinking anxious, critical, fearful, negative thoughts, if you are in the habit of thinking negatively, you will just keep doing it over and over again. But don't misunderstand me, I don't meant this is something you're doing on purpose. No, not at all. Rather it's just a poor mental habit that you probably picked up during childhood. But because you're unaware of what you're doing, you just keep doing it over and over. And this unfortunately means you also get to keep experiencing the consequences of your own negative thinking over and over again too!

But don't despair. Now by understanding the law of substitution, you have the key to changing these poor mental habits into better ones. Once you see what you're doing, you can use this law to change your poor mental habits even if it does take time and effort. Now that you understand the law, every time you catch yourself thinking negatively, you know you can change the drift of your thinking by substituting new thoughts for the old negative ones!

The key is in your hand.

The choice is yours!

Since you are the only thinker in your mind, it's all up to you.

What to do in practice

As I've said before, the first step is recognizing your general mental habits. It's hard to change something if you aren't aware of what you're doing in the first place. So watch yourself carefully until you can see exactly what's going on. And then make up your mind to replace negative thoughts every time they arise with new positive ones. Armed with an understanding of the law of substitution, you now know that you can turn the movement of your thoughts in a new direction by replacing one thought pattern with another thought pattern. It's really very simple once you understand the mechanism. And because this is mechanical law, this is truly the scientific way to deal with any negative thought patterns or conditions in your life. You simply build the opposite thoughts and resulting conditions into your consciousness by substituting one thought pattern with another.

So you can now see that the law of substitution is indeed a very important tool when it comes to being the choice-maker in your life and taking control of your mind. If you understand this mechanism, you have the key to mastering your mind and changing your thought patterns, no matter how negative they may be at the present moment.

An experiment

If you are in doubt as to whether you can change your life by using the law of substitution and changing your thinking, try this experiment.

Decide that for one whole week, you are going to think negatively about everything that happens to you. No matter what, you are going to be critical and find fault with every situation and every person you meet—and you are going to find fault with yourself as well. This means that by using the law of substitution, every time you think something good and positive, you are going to replace the thought with a critical negative thought. Do this for a week and see what happens. See what your life looks and feels like when you do this.

Then take the next week and decide that you are going to think positively and kindly about everything that happens to you. No matter what happens, you are going to see the potential in every situation and every person you meet during this week. This means that by using the law of substitution, every time you have a negative or critical thought about a person or a situation or even about yourself, you will immediately replace it with a good, kind and positive thought. Do this for a week and see what happens. See what your life looks and feels like when you do this.

If a week is too long for you, you can do this experiment for two days instead of two weeks. On the first day, be negative about everything no matter what—and on the second day, be positive about everything no matter what. And see what happens. See what those two days look and feel like... See what your experience is...

For your health

You can also use the great law of substitution to improve your health. When you are sick or feeling low in the loafers, every time you think a negative thought about your body and your health, replace it with a wonderful, positive thought like "my body is a great, powerful healing machine!" Or any other statement or affirmation that feels right to you. So instead of dwelling on what's wrong with you when you're feeling ill, substitute powerful thoughts for any weak, sick thoughts you may be having. Say things to yourself like "my immune system is strong and healthy and is dealing effectively with this situation now".

Law 10: THE LAW OF MENTAL EQUIVALENTS

Like attracts like

The techniques in many of today's popular self-help books and modern mental training programs are based on the law of mental equivalents. This law explains that everything we experience in the outer world is a reflection of the mental equivalents we hold in thought.

When we understand this mechanism, we also understand that we must have the mental equivalent of whatever "Good" we wish to experience in the outer, external plane before we can experience it. Of course this is just another way of saying that *thought is cause and experience is effect,* but it is a very useful and practical way of looking at and understanding this mechanism.

So let's look at little more closely at what this means.

The law of mental equivalents means, for example, that you cannot and will not experience the abundance of life in your life until you have a prosperity consciousness. When you have the mental equivalent of abundance, in other words when you think abundant thoughts and feel abundant, when you see and understand that all the wealth of the world belongs to you, you will experience prosperity in your life whether or not you have money in the bank. Prosperity, like everything else in life, is a state of mind. But of course, we have been brought up to believe the opposite. We have been raised to believe that you can only feel prosperous if you have money in the bank. But look around you. Is that true? Don't you know a lot of people who have money in the bank and don't feel prosperous? So is it true that you can only feel prosperous if you have money in the bank? If you are in doubt, take the time to go inside and find out if this is really true for you. Or is the opposite in fact true? What exactly do you mean by prosperity?

And what about the other areas of your life? What about love? If you want love, can you get it? As we all know, it usually doesn't work like that. In fact, wanting something badly usually pushes it away from us, because the very act of wanting is actually an affirmation that we don't have it! And this holds true for love too. Especially since love is our nature! Interestingly enough, the law of mental equivalents tells us that if we want to experience love in our lives and in our relationships, the best way to do this is to realize the love that is within us and cultivate it! Because everything "out there" is just reflecting back to us what we have "in here". All our experiences in the so-called outer world are merely equivalents or reflections of our inner states of mind or consciousness. So be the love you want to experience. Cultivate a love consciousness!

> Be the love you want to experience.

Take a moment and think about this. Of course you want to experience love, but do you have a love consciousness? Or do you see critical people and enemies everywhere you turn? And are you critical yourself? Take a look within and find out. Watch your thinking and see if you are the love you want to experience. Watching like this may come as a shock because we are so often completely unaware of our own thought patterns and under-lying beliefs (see Law 8, the Law of Underlying Beliefs). We don't see that even though we want love, we are often sending out angry and critical thoughts, which as we now can see, will be reflected back to us. Understanding the mental laws and the mechanisms they describe, will help you unlock the key to your own behavior and experiences.

Like attracts like

Another way of stating this law is: *Like attracts like*. If you don't believe me, start to observe the people around you. Try picking one of your friends for example and then try to ascertain the general climate of your friend's thoughts—his or her state of mind. Is the climate warm and friendly or cold and critical? Is it light-hearted and free or closed and depressed? If you watch closely, you will discover that interestingly enough, people's experiences match their states of mind perfectly. And you will see that angry people often have many experiences to be angry about! Since they have an angry or irritated mindset, angry or irritating things just show up! And the people who are truly kind and loving, what are their experiences? Try thinking of someone who has a truly generous mindset—then look at his or her life experience. Do they match? If you start to notice, you will probably see that people who are generous, loving and kind seem to meet evidence of the loving kindness they embody wherever they go. And this goes for people who have that very special prosperity vibe too. And for people who have that dynamic, healthy, energetic vibe. Can you see how their life experiences match and reflect back their mentalities? It's interesting to watch isn't it?

It's the same for you

Of course it's the same with you. So please watch yourself and find out whether this is true or not. Just notice what happens. On a day when you wake up cross and irritated, doesn't everything just seem to go wrong? And then when you wake up and your energy is high—well what happens then? Watch and see and I guarantee you will soon understand why the Wise say "exaltation is a magnet for all Good". When you know the mechanism, you understand that joy and laughter, elation, exhilaration, rapture, excitement, bliss are states of mind that attract every Good thing in this universe. They must because the universe is just reflecting back what's in here. Nothing else is going on.

If you don't believe this is true, try this experiment. Make a mental note of when Good things happen to you and you will discover they happen when you're in an elevated state of mind. And extraordinary things happen when you're in a joyful or exalted state of mind—or in love...

> Your present experience always reflects
> your present state of mind.

Mental techniques

Mental techniques such as affirmations and visualization exercises are based on this law. Both techniques aim to break our old negative programming and help us develop new mental patterns and new mental equivalents. By means of constant repetition, we can change the groove of our thinking and begin to entertain new thought patterns. When this happens, events and experiences in the outer world begin reflecting our new thought patterns back to us.

The prayer of gratitude is one of the strongest types of mental affirmations. By giving thanks for all the good you already have in your life, you set in motion the unfolding of wonders and miracles in your life because *like attracts like*. When you know this, it makes life very simple because it means to have a wonderful life your most important task is to keep your mental energy high. And as I said above, high states of mental energy include the praiseful, exalted and grateful states of mind. Nothing else is as important as this.

Mind can't see things it doesn't believe!
You have to believe it before you can see it!

Questioning catastrophic thinking

Of course if you discover that the climate of your thinking is dark and negative and that you often are plagued by catastrophic thinking, I suggest you make a dedicated effort to identify your negative thoughts and then to hold them up to the light of truth by questioning them. This is another important way of dissolving our old negative programming and allowing the true goodness that we are to emerge and rule our lives. (For detailed instructions on how to question your negative thinking, see the section on Investigation tools on page 132).

Law 11: THE LAW OF TRUTH

No thoughts are true

By contemplating the mental laws, we have now begun to see how the mechanics of creation work. *Thoughts arising, world arising.* This is the core experience, this is the mechanism of this thing we call life. And in this book, I have been trying to slow things down enough (at least conceptually), so that we can catch a glimpse of this mechanism, become aware of it, and see it unfolding. And as we do, we begin to see that as thoughts arise, so does our world.

This is the way of it.

To know exactly what I am talking about, think back to a morning when you woke up a total blank. It happens on occasion so I am sure you have experienced it. You wake up and you know you are awake but there is no thought and no world. You are blank. You can't remember who you are or where you are or even what you are. And then, in a split second, it all comes back to you. The thoughts come tumbling in and your world appears. You are this person, in this bed, with this mate besides you. You have to get up and take a shower and eat breakfast and go to work. And with these thoughts pouring in, your world appears again. This is it. And our entire life experience is like this—only we usually don't notice. We usually don't see it happening because it happens so fast. But this is all that is going on—thought/world appears simultaneously. Before thought, no world, thought arising, world arising.

If you make yourself very, very still and very, very quiet, you may be able to catch a glimpse of this, which is what meditation is about. Just watching, not interfering, not wanting anything in particular, just being aware. Can you see the thoughts as they come and go? Here comes a thought—and then—there it goes again. And then another. And another. Mind bubbling like a well within you, creating a "this" and a "that"—a supermarket, a bicycle, a bus stop, and infinite worlds and stars and experiences... all for your delight and amusement.

The impermanence of it

When we can see this—that thoughts arise and disappear like this—we can also see that thoughts must be impermanent since they come and go. We see that thoughts are like the wind, here, there and then gone again. There is nothing to them. No substance. So they cannot be real. No. They cannot and are not real. Thoughts are not reality. They are, well, just thoughts! And this is how and why we can know that *no thoughts are true*. Or should I say, by observing this we come to understand that no thoughts can be true. It's just the bubbling well of mind. Bubbling. And then a thought comes. And another. And the thought is a mental construct, naming that which cannot be named. The thought is putting a label or labels on the field—on the Absolute or Ultimate Reality in which there are no distinctions or dichotomies. Which is why thoughts—all thoughts—are untrue. Mind bubbles up about "this" or about "that" and what does this have to do with reality? What does this thought or any other thought have to do with the always stable ground of beingness which is altogether beyond words and altogether present? But of course, until we "get" (understand, grasp) this, we don't "get" it and we identify with our thoughts and think this is reality. But the truth is—*reality is not what we think*. What we think is just thoughts, concepts, mental constructions we use for convenience at best. But despite the convenience, they are still unreal and therefore untrue.

Reality is not what we think.

You can say all thoughts are just relative positions in the greater whole—but no thought is Absolute truth since Absolute truth cannot be told or named. Reality, the real, is beyond all this. Beyond explaining, beyond understanding, beyond our ability to conceptualize. This might sound mystical or mysterious, but this reality is not mystical, mysterious or far-fetched in any way. In fact, it's right here, right in front of our noses, right now. *It is this. This. This. All of this.*

So let us keep our minds focused on this line of reasoning—until we are clear enough to see that there is reality—and then there are our thoughts. And that these two phenomena are two completely different things. In other words, they are not one and the same. It's very important to understand this. To understand that Reality is the unmoving, always stable, *this.* And then there are our thoughts, the ever-changing, bubbling well of thoughts arising and disappearing. And we—our so-called individual life experiences—are these thoughts.

Attaching to thought

And now we come to a key observation: *All suffering arises from identifying with (or believing in) thoughts that are not true! All suffering is attachment to thoughts.*

Since we now know that no thoughts are true, we come to see that the root cause of all our suffering is *believing what we think. If we didn't believe what we think, it would be impossible to suffer.*

This is so mind-boggling an observation that I will repeat it... *If we didn't believe what we think, it would be impossible to suffer.*

How can we know this? Well ask yourself. If you didn't believe what you think, what would be left?

Without believing our thoughts, all that would be left is *what*

85

is. And that would be reality. And since reality is nothing (nothing) we can conceptualize, we cannot in any way label it "good" or "bad"... and without the "good" or "bad" label, how can we suffer?

All suffering is mental and arises when the mind adds the label and then we believe what we think. We say this is "bad", "wrong" and then we get to live it. You could say that when we believe our thoughts, it is like we are putting an artificial matrix of ideas on top of reality. And you could also say — so what? And yes, that is true — so what... Problems only arise when our matrix (thoughts) and reality don't fit together. When they don't match, that's when we suffer. Because in that moment, when our thoughts don't match reality, we are resisting reality, we are resisting what is — we are resisting the way things are. And when that happens, we always lose. Because *reality is what it is.* We don't get a say in this. We don't have any power over what is. What is, in this moment, already is. It's already happened. It's here now, done. And again, it's not a question of "good" or "bad", "right" or "wrong", it's simply a question of *what is.*

So I repeat... *Resistance to reality is the only suffering. Resistance to this moment is the only suffering.* (Suffering in the past is just a thought in your mind because the past is already over — and suffering in the future is also just a thought in your mind because the future is also just a thought.)

So we suffer when our thoughts (the artificial matrix we superimpose) and reality (this moment) don't match. We suffer when our thoughts and reality turn out to be two different things. And this is *always* the case.

If you can understand this, really understand this, you can live a happy life, regardless of what is going on in your life, regardless of outer circumstances, regardless of what your body is doing... regardless. This is the secret of the very Wise. They have *seen* reality and they know that *reality is not what they think.* So they don't believe their thoughts. They don't believe what they think! They know that *no thoughts are true.*

* * *

But even though reality is not something we can conceptualize, reality is something we can *experience directly.*

Why?

Because reality is what we are, what is, right now—beyond explaining—beyond understanding—beyond thought. *It is this. This. This.*

In conclusion

To summarize what we have learned in Part 1, we can say:

1. The nature of mind is that thoughts arise and disappear.

2. There is often a difference between reality and our thinking.

3. There is a cause-and-effect relationship between our thinking and our experience. Thought is cause, experience is effect.

4. Unhappiness and suffering arise when our thinking is out of harmony with reality. In other words, we suffer when our thinking (thoughts) and reality do not match.

5. We can end our unhappiness and suffering (and experience more peace and happiness) by bringing our thinking back into harmony with reality.

But the big question of course is how? How do we bring our thinking back into harmony with reality? What does "bring our thinking back into harmony with reality" actually mean and how do we do this in practice—most specifically and concretely? That is what the next section of this book is about.

PART TWO: PRACTICE

USING THE POWER OF MIND WISELY

The incredible power of mind

Now that we know that all our experiences are mental experiences, we can begin to understand the incredible power of mind. So with this understanding of mind, let us examine how we can begin to use this power more wisely—because this is the big issue. It's really not a question of whether or not we are creating our own experiences of reality, because we are. Rather it is a question of how we are doing it and *what experiences* we are creating. Because like it or not, we *are* creating our experiences every moment of every day.

For most of us, this process, the way our thoughts create our experiences, has been an unconscious process until now. But now we are waking up. Now we are beginning to catch brief glimpses and actually see how this process works. We are beginning to see the mechanism... and it's fascinating. Fascinating because this understanding is not just mind-boggling, it's also very *empowering*. With this new understanding, we begin to realize that we actually do have a choice. We actually do have a choice in each and every now moment as to how we are going to use the incredible mind power that has been given us. Are we just going to habitually fall into our old programming? And keep repeating the same old negative, stressful thoughts and patterns? Or are we going to be mindful and observe what's going in our minds and then use the full power that is given us to step back and question the validity of our thoughts? Are we going to ask ourselves if the thoughts we are dwelling upon and entertaining are in anyway true? Especially now that we know that whatever we are thinking and believing with conviction, we are also projecting and thus experiencing in our lives... as our life.

If you are reading this book, I know that the answer to this question is already *yes!* You've already made up your mind and you're ready. Ready for the best game in town! Because yes, this mind game is the best, most amazing game in town. Quite simply because *it's the only game in town* and because *it's the game of your life!* So nothing could be more important or more exciting. And once you get the hang of it, nothing can possibly be more rewarding either. To see and understand the way your mind works and to realize what this understanding means for you.

Because it means *you can change!* It means *you can live a happy life now — no matter what your life circumstances are!* Now I realize this is a challenging statement — but it is true nevertheless. But don't believe me! Test everything I say in this book for yourself and see if it's true. All I can tell you is that in my experience, it is true.

One thing I do know is that every single person alive wants to know how to live a happy life. I've been many places and talked to many, many people and everyone says the same. Everyone wants the same. *We all want to live happy lives no matter what our life circumstances are. No matter how young, old, healthy, sick, rich, poor, we are. And we want to live these happy lives right here, right now. That's everyone's deepest desire. That's what everyone wants. You, me and everyone else. We're all the same. We all want the same. To experience the happiness, the infinite goodness, that we all know is our birthright.*

And now you can do it. Now you have the key to living a happy life in your hands. Because only you can decide how you are going to use the incredible power of mind that has been given to you.

That's the deal. You're the master, whether you know it or not. And isn't that just wonderful, and lovely, and incredible, and doesn't that mean that your life — and everyone else's life — is an amazing adventure? Because what will you do next? What will you choose next? You never know until you do it.

So let's look more closely at our choices.

Let's look more closely at the many ways we can choose to use the power of our minds a bit more wisely.

Mind tools

I call the techniques and focal points described in this section of the book "mind tools". And by this I mean the ways and means by which we can direct and/or question our thoughts so that our thoughts are more in harmony with reality and the way things are. And since the Nature of Reality, the way things are, is equal, identical, and interchangeable with the Good that we seek, the result is the happy life we long for becomes ours. It might sound complicated, but it's really very simple. In fact it's so simple that most of us just don't get it.

And even if we do get it, it's not always so easy to put this understanding into practice because putting these techniques into practice requires self-discipline, which can be pretty challenging! For most of us, learning to choose more wisely in every now moment means constant vigilance. We have to be awake to do it!

It takes practice

So it is important to remember that everything we are going to be looking at in this section of the book takes practice. It doesn't just happen automatically. Most people don't just wake up and get it (although a few actually do). In this connection, it's interesting to notice that people are accustomed to working with their bodies, but not with their minds. By this I mean it is accepted knowledge that you have to have self-discipline and work with your body if you want to get in shape, lose weight, live a healthy life, be a dancer, an athlete, or just an ordinary person who's fit and healthy. Everyone knows and understands this. Everyone accepts that taking care of our bodies requires work and discipline. But very few people understand that the same goes for our minds. But the truth is if you want to live a happy life, you have to *work with your mind.* It just doesn't happen automatically—at least not for anyone I know!

As you start waking up, you begin to understand that working with your mind is more important than anything else you can do in this life. In fact, it's the most important thing of all, especially if you want to live a happy life! And since that's what this book is about—*understanding the way our minds work and using this information to live a happy life*—it is important to understand that all the mind tools we are going to be looking at require self-discipline and practice. It's not enough to just read about these techniques, you have to work with them on a daily basis to achieve results.

I mention this because I often notice when I do private sessions with people that they don't have a daily practice. When I ask someone, what is your daily practice, many people just look at me with surprise. Oh yes they've read a lot of books and been to a lot of lectures and workshops, but when it comes to a concrete daily practice, it turns out that most people don't do anything. They just expect that they are going to feel better because they've read a few good books and gone to a few lectures. But it doesn't work like that. Real change requires dedication and practice. Real change requires devotion to your cause. Real change requires self-discipline and practice, practice, practice. (See suggestions for a daily program on page 167).

> If you want to live a happy life,
> it's infinitely more important
> to work with your mind
> than to work with your body.

Two types of mind tools

There are many types of mind tools, many wonderful techniques you can use when you understand the mental laws and the way the mind works. To simplify matters, I have divided the tools into two groups—*focus tools* and *investigation tools*.

I like to think of these two different types of tools as the two wings of a bird. You can't fly with just one wing; you need both wings to do it. It's the same with these two groups of tools. It's hard to fly with only one group, but a combination of the two can give amazing results. So let's look at what I mean by the two types of tools.

Focus tools are techniques that are based on the understanding that what we focus our attention on grows in our experience. (See Law 5: The Law of Focus on page 48 which says we experience whatever we focus our attention on). Thus all focus tools are techniques that help us direct the focus of our attention wisely. They help us focus on the real, on this moment, on the goodness of reality that is right here right before our eyes. They help us focus on the happiness which is our true nature, and on the Nature of Reality itself, which is boundless love and the Good that we seek.

Investigation tools are techniques that help us identify, question, and lessen our attachment to the negative thoughts and beliefs that are blocking our experience of the goodness of life that is here and now. With investigation tools, we can examine the negative programming we have received and release ourselves from the nightmare of our own stressful thinking.

So with these two types of techniques, we can build a daily practice in which we focus on the goodness that is already ours and which we want to experience more of while questioning and releasing any negative thoughts and beliefs that are blocking our experience of this goodness.

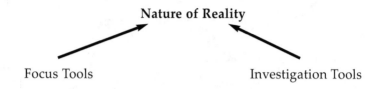

Nature of Reality

Focus Tools   Investigation Tools

The 2 wings of the bird,
each brings you back
to the Nature of Reality

FOCUS TOOLS

Every thought is an affirmation

With our new understanding of the way the mind works and the cause and effect relationship between thoughts and our experience, we can now understand that every thought we believe is an affirmation. And especially every thought we think and believe with conviction is a very powerful affirmation. So it turns out that we are all saying affirmations constantly every day of our lives when we tell our stories of what life is. We say "life is like this" and then we get to live it. We say "this is bad" and we get to experience it. We say "she shouldn't do that" and we get to experience the stress that thought brings.

This means that we are all masters when it comes to saying affirmations. No one is better at saying affirmations than anyone else. We are all equal when it comes to experiencing our thinking and our beliefs! And there's no mystery about it either. So if you previously believed that affirmations were some magical statements you could say which would change your life, you now know that this was just a misunderstanding, an innocent misconception. The fact is you have been saying affirmations all your life—and you have been experiencing the effects of your beliefs all your life. Nothing else is going on. So all you have to do if you want to know what your affirmations are is to look at what you are thinking and saying over and over again with conviction. These are your affirmations. So the real question is—what are you affirming! Do you really want to experience what you are believing and saying with conviction? Does what you are affirming have anything to do with reality? In other words, are your thoughts and beliefs true? Do they match the goodness of life that is available to you right now? Do they match what is actually going on in front of your eyes right here and right now — or are you somewhere off in fantasy land, projecting horror stories that are making you suffer for no reason at all?

If that's the case, if you have looked at your thinking and beliefs and found that they are way off the beam and causing you unnecessary suffering, the simple focus tools described in this section will help you bring your thinking and your belief systems back into harmony with reality. And when that happens, you can begin to notice and enjoy the goodness of life that is yours, right here and right now.

Gratitude

One of the best focus tools of all is gratitude, quite simply because thoughts of gratitude are the best thoughts of all! Why are thoughts of gratitude the best thoughts of all? Because life is a gift! And feeling gratitude brings you closer to the truth about life. It's as simple as that. Life, this amazing thing we call life, has simply been given to us! And it's ours! The gift of life! And we've done absolutely nothing to deserve it. It's simply beyond comprehension when we actually try to understand that we have *life*! That life is ours. That we are alive. Living, breathing, being, right now today, right this very moment. Unfortunately, most of us are so busy running around like chickens without our heads that we rarely, if ever, notice that we have been given the gift of life.

What have we done to deserve this?

What have you done to deserve this?

What have I done to deserve this?

What have any of us done?

It's beyond doing, isn't it?

It's beyond mind-boggling.

Look, here I am. Look, there you are! Look! There is this. *This!* Sitting here. *This. This!* With this body, this mind, these fingers typing away at this keyboard to you whoever or whatever you are that is reading this… it is just beyond comprehension. Isn't it? And not only that, it's such an adventure too. Can you see that? Can you feel it? Deep inside you? Can you see the amazing way it's been set up for us so that everything—and I mean everything—is happening for us. Can you see that now? How it is all unfolding just for you? And that you haven't done anything whatsoever to deserve it and you don't have any idea what it is or where it's going. And you don't even know what's going to happen a minute from now even though we like to think we do. But in reality, do we? So it's always an adventure for us, isn't it? We're always in the middle of a great adventure. And then it changes again… So yes, grateful thoughts, the prayer of gratitude, the song of gratitude, the melody of gratitude, however you find it, however you sing it or express it… go there and do it! It's your birthright we're talking about here, the reason why you want to live, the thing that makes your heart sing, the mystery, the magic, the melody, the love, the joy… Gratitude is the open door to all of it. Gratitude! But only you can walk through the door of gratitude for you.

Focus tool no. 1: Gratitude lists

Here's the world's fastest and easiest way to pick up your spirits and make yourself feel good—make a gratitude list. If you wake up feeling blue, well take out a piece of paper and start writing down all the things you are grateful for in your life. Start small. Start with the simple things. Write "I am grateful for" at the top of the page and start with things like:

I am alive
I have food in my refrigerator
I can walk
I can see
I can hear
I can talk

I have a nice place to sleep
My bed is so comfortable
I have a good apartment
I have a beautiful window here with trees outside
There is heat in my apartment
I have running water in the bathroom and a nice shower
I have a job to go to
I have money in the bank
I have clothes to wear
I have even more clothes in my closet
I have several pairs of shoes to choose between
I live in a country where there is peace and prosperity
I have a telephone and a television and a cell phone
I have people I can talk to
I have a nice view from my window
The sun is shining today
It's spring and the birds are chirping outside
The flowers are lovely
There is a beautiful tree over there
My dog is wagging his tail
I have my own computer
I have wonderful children to play with
I have a best friend
She is so supportive
I can call her when I need to talk and she listens
I have other friends too
My friend Anne is so understanding
My ...

Well once you get started, well the list just goes on and on. And if you do this on a daily basis, I guarantee it will change the "tone" of your day and your life. But again, making gratitude lists is not just something to think about. You have to actually do it—even if it seems a little silly and so very simple. It's the doing that counts. So sit down with a piece of paper and give it a try.

Focus tool no. 2: Power questions

Another simple but powerful technique to help you develop gratitude and learn to focus on the good in your life is to ask questions that empower you. You can make up your own questions, but here are Anthony Robbins five power questions just to give you the idea. If you want to get your day off to a good start, write these questions on a piece of paper and put them by your bed. When the alarm clock rings in the morning, start your day by answering the five questions. Find at least three answers for each question.

Anthony Robbins' Five Morning Questions:
"1. What am I proud of in my life?
2. What am I grateful for?
3. Who loves me and who do I love?
4. What's great about my present situation?
5. What can I do today to make my life better?"

The reason it's a good idea to ask these questions in the morning is because the morning is where we set the "tone" for our day. That's why the morning is also a good place to notice the mental climate of your mind. If you don't understand what I mean, make a mental note to notice your first thoughts upon waking every morning for the next five days. I say this is because if you make a mental note to notice your first thoughts in the morning when you wake up, you will discover that you always think the same thing every single morning. And that's actually how you are setting the "tone" for your day. So take a good look at your first morning thoughts and find out what you are doing! You can try writing down your first morning thoughts for five days in a row and see what you're thinking and if you always think the same thing when you wake up in the morning. It can be pretty revealing.

Is the first thing you think when you wake up:

- Oh what a wonderful day! I am so thankful to be alive. Life is such a great adventure!
- I can't wait to see what's going to happen today. I know something good is going to happen to me today.
- Oh damn, there goes the alarm and I just fell asleep. I'm more tired now than when I went to bed. I don't know how I'm going to get through another day.
- Oh no, not another day at that stupid place. I hate my job and know I'm wasting my life and my talent there.
- Oh no, everything hurts… why is my life like this?
- Oh how lucky I am to be alive! I can't wait to tell my partner how much I love him (her) and to hug my kids. I am truly blessed.

If you discover that your first thoughts are not setting the best "tone" for your day, try answering the five morning questions every morning for at least 10 days in a row to help you establish a more positive morning mental pattern. And then see how your life changes!

Another good way to use these power questions is to do a "telephone chain" with them. Here's what to do. Get together four or five people who want to work together to lift their energy and make a telephone chain using the five power questions. The chain works like this: Jane calls Tom and asks him the five questions which he answers, then Tom calls Mary and asks Mary the five questions which she answers, then Mary calls Susan and asks Susan the five questions which she answers, then Susan calls Jane and asks Jane the five questions which she now answers. Agree to do this exercise at a specific time each day—preferably the same time for example at 10 am in the morning. Do it for a whole week and see how you and your friends feel. It's great fun.

Focus tool no. 3: Notice the support

Here's another good technique I learned from Byron Katie. She calls it "noticing the support". Noticing the support is a great way to relax, lift your energy, and help you feel safe and at home in the world.

Here's what you do: Sit quietly in a comfortable chair and close your eyes. Then start noticing how everything is supporting you right this very minute. Start by noticing how the chair itself is supporting your body. Feel your weight on the chair and notice how firmly and nicely the chair is holding you. Then notice how the floor under the chair is holding and supporting the chair and how comfortably your feet are resting on the floor and how the floor is holding your feet and you and the chair so firmly. And then notice how the whole room you are sitting in is made for you. How the floor and the walls and all the furniture are all for you. And how this room is in this building which was built to support this room where you are sitting so comfortably and how it is all for you. All of it supporting you. And notice how your body is there for you, your heart and your lungs and your arms and your legs and your digestion—the whole marvelous network of skin and bones and organs all for you. All to support you, to give you life itself. Notice how your heart beats for you. How it supports you by sending blood throughout your body. And then there are your lungs and the air that moves in and out of your body. So nicely and comfortably supporting life perfectly in you right here and right now. And what about your hands and arms, these marvelous limbs that work so tirelessly for you, helping you do things and making life so interesting. And what about your legs and feet that take you places and help you get from here to there and back again—all supporting you? The whole system, the whole network. Your body, the chair, the floor, the room, the building—all made for you. All supporting you. And what about the street outside and the city you live in. Think about how it supports you. Everyone out there working to make life function in this marvelous city. People bringing food to the supermarkets, newspaper boys bringing you the news, doctors and nurses ready to take care of you at the hospital should you need help, policemen making sure traffic flows smoothly... is there anything out there that is not supporting you? ... And so it goes. The more you think about, the more you elaborate on it, the more you can see how everything and everyone is supporting you. In fact all of life is supporting you. This earth supporting you, this planet in this solar system in this galaxy in this universe. All for you. All making this moment possible for you. Isn't it just amazing? So take a time out—and notice the support. This is a wonderful, calming exercise you can do on a daily basis. It will help make you realize how truly *at home* you are in this world.

Focus tool no. 4: What it takes to eat my breakfast

Here's another spin on the exercise above that I developed. I call it my "what it takes to eat my breakfast" exercise. And here's how it goes:

I am sitting here at the breakfast table and in front of me is my plate with a fried egg and some slices of fried tomato. I also have a bagel with cream cheese and apricot jam plus a glass of orange juice and a cup of green tea. Sometimes when I sit with this wonderful breakfast before me, I like to think what it took to bring this food to me this morning. First I think about the chicken who laid the eggs and the farmer who has the chicken farm and also the farmer who cultivated the tomatoes and the farmer who planted and harvested the grain for my bagel. Then I think about the good earth on which these farms are located and I think about what it takes for farms like these to produce these chickens and tomatoes and grains. And then I think of the good soil that everything grows on and the sun, the moon, the heavens, the earth, and the rain—until I see that the whole universe of elements is required for me to eat this egg and tomato and bagel. And then I think about the farm itself, the buildings, the farm machinery, and all the people who work on these farms and the whole business of their nourishing and harvesting these eggs and tomatoes and grains just for me. And then I think about all the people involved in designing, developing and making the farm machinery and the buildings. Next I consider the whole network of people who are working to bring this wonderful produce to the marketplace and get it to the supermarkets including my supermarket... and all the people who are working in the super-markets... and what it has taken to create and nourish all these people and their parents and their families and who gave birth to who and ... When I finish considering this, I then think about how I have this wonderful kitchen where I can cook my eggs and toast my bagel. I also consider the lovely white dishes I have to put the food on and the nice silverware I have and the beautiful tea cup and all the people and materials and processes involved just so I could have these beautiful dishes... and well as you can see, once I get started, I realize that the whole universe and everything single thing in it has come together so that I could eat my breakfast. Take one thing away and I couldn't be sitting here eating this breakfast could I? It's truly amazing to consider how the whole universe is involved in making my breakfast, isn't it? And this leads us (once again) to the truly mind-boggling discovery that *everything is connected to everything else* and that *this is like this because that is like that.* Thus we see that there are no independent, separate happenings anywhere. Nothing is standing alone. Nothing *can* stand alone. Everything, all of it including us, is part of the one field, which leads us right back to the Ultimate Reality, the non-dual field that is all of it, which is what we are.

So now you can see that this very simple morning exercise is actually high spiritual practice, because it always leads you to the Ultimate Reality, the truth about this thing called life.

But again, this simple exercise will only work for you if *you actually do it.* It's not enough to just read about it here. You must actually take the time to slow down the wheels of mind enough so that you can actually reflect on and *see* what is really going on. Only in this way will you be able to get a deeper realization of how it is all one, wonderful interconnected web of life that is all for you!

It's called *waking up to reality!*

Meditation

Meditation is one of the most important tools available to us. So let's look at what meditation is and why it is so important.

First of all, understanding what meditation is…

In this book, we have been examining consciousness and the way our minds work. And one of the most important things we've discovered is that thoughts arise and disappear and that this is going on all the time. As we begin to look inward, at what is going on in our minds, we are often shocked and dismayed to discover just how fast all this is going on—how fast thoughts arise and disappear—and also at how much totally ridiculous mental jabber we constantly have. Our minds are just churning and churning. And when you discover this your first reaction might be "it's a zoo in there!" And yes, you're right—it is a zoo in there! Your own private zoo! The other thing you discover, when you begin watching your mind, is how most of the time you attach to the various thoughts and stories that arise and then run off to somewhere in dreamland in the past or the future. And if you keep watching what you're doing, you begin to realize the shocking truth, which is that you actually spend very little time in the present moment! The truth is you're mostly off in dreamland somewhere (whether you're awake or asleep). This is a big discovery and a very important one. Discovering that we're just not here! Discovering we're just not awake to this moment. No. We spend most of our time being everywhere else in our minds, thinking about this and worrying about that, but we're almost never present here and now. And when we're not conscious of the present moment, it really means we're not conscious at all! We're just lost in our stories. (Oh yes, we might be conscious beings but when we're lost in our stories, we're not conscious that we're conscious! And we're not aware that we are present in this moment.)

And you see friend, being present, being conscious here and now is what waking up to reality is all about! Because reality is this moment. That's what reality is. Reality is right here in front of our noses. Reality is *this*. Reality is *now*. Reality is *here*. Reality is the only moment that exists.

And why would you want to miss this? The only place the happiness you seek can be experienced, the only place the happiness you are can be lived. It's here and now. The radiance that is *this*. The radiance that is *you*.

And this is where meditation comes in. Because quite simply, in its most basic form, meditation is about coming back to this moment. That's what meditation is. Meditation is about being aware now. Meditation is being here, being present, in this now moment. That's what meditation is. Meditation is sitting quietly, doing nothing and watching. Being awake. Being aware. Watching your mind run off and then bringing yourself back to this moment. That's about it. That's meditation. It couldn't be simpler and it couldn't be more difficult. Meditation is probably the easiest and the hardest thing in the world to do. If you don't believe me, just trying sitting quietly and looking at a blank wall for 10 minutes and being present in each now moment. It's almost impossible to do isn't it? The minute you sit down, your mind goes galloping off! So it takes effort and self-discipline to sit down and keep bringing yourself back to this moment. To stay awake and keep coming back to now, to reality.

So yes, meditate!

So yes, make up your mind to meditate. Make it your intention to meditate. And do it on a daily basis.

But start small (rather than starting big and giving up after a few days) and keep at it. Make it a regular practice. Do it at the same time every day. Start with 10 minutes a day. Then move on to 15 when that feels comfortable and soon you will find you can sit quietly and do nothing for 20 minutes at a time.

But what's the point, you ask?

Why should I do this? Why should I waste my precious time sitting quietly doing nothing when there is so much to do, so much to accomplish and achieve?

And all I can reply is yes dear, there goes the mind again. Busy making plans and pulling us off in another direction and constantly telling us that being present in this moment is not that important! Which brings up the whole question of what this whole thing called life is all about. Because really, what is it all about? This constant chase for happiness somewhere out there in the future if we just can perform well enough. Which I now have come to see is really such a cruel way to live our lives. Because we never allow ourselves to experience the absolute bliss, the absolute joy, of being totally present right now—without any thought of accomplishing anything or becoming anything or going anywhere or doing anything at all. And then we die! It's really so cruel!

So yes, meditate!

Give yourself the gift! Allow it to happen.

Be here now.

Be good to you!

Savor this moment. Do it for you!

Make up your mind to sit down and breathe and just let everything be as it is. Make the choice to do it. To pull back and let everything be. And just be present and watch.

Now you can also say that this decision to be aware in this moment, is a decision we can make in every now moment—and not just when we sit down to meditate. And yes, this is also true. We *can* also make the decision to be present in every now moment, but most of us can't or don't do this. It's too difficult because our minds (and our lives) are just too busy. And that is why practicing meditation can help. Meditation is the formal moment—the formal decision—when you say to yourself, ok I'm going to sit down now for 10 or 20 minutes and focus my attention on being present now, on being aware of this moment. Meditation is the formal act. And as you practice doing this every day at the designated time, you discover that you are cultivating the ability (the awareness) to be present. And then, sooner or later, this will begin to spill over into your whole life. So yes, meditate. Yes, cultivate the ability to be aware in this moment. Practice being conscious of this moment. Because it does take practice. It doesn't just happen automatically. So keep making the decision—over and over again—to actually see what is happening right in front of your nose, right now. And keep making the decision, over and over again. And keep sitting there and keep bringing yourself back to this moment, over and over again. And keep coming back to now and experiencing this moment, this happening, this reality, this *whatever it is*, now.

When you do this, you are meditating, whether you are sitting formally or not.

> Only you can make the choice to bring yourself back
> to this moment.

It can only happen now

So it's really very simple. There is only one place you can wake up to reality—and it's here. There is only one time you can wake up to reality—and it's now. And why is this so? Because everything else is just a thought in your mind.

Waking up to reality—can only happen now, because now is all there is, in reality. Everything else is a dream, an illusion, a passing thought. But *this, this now, this* is it! This is reality. Meditation means coming back to *this*. Meditation means being aware of *this*. *Being present now.*

About other techniques

There is quite a bit of confusion when it comes to the word *meditation*. So I would just like to point out here that when I talk about *meditation,* I am not talking about relaxation exercises (which are excellent for relaxing) and I am not talking about visualization exercises (which are excellent for visualizing and achieving specific results). Nor am I talking about channeling (which is fine if you are into channeling). Nor am I talking about focusing on specific objects like a Buddha statue or a flower or a candle or dwelling on specific subjects like love or compassion or impermanence (all of which are fine if this is what you want to focus on). In this section, I am only talking about meditation in the strictest, most traditional sense of the word. I am talking about meditation as an awareness practice—as a practice of sitting quietly in this now moment and simply being present. That is what I mean when I use the word meditation.

How to sit

Since we are looking at "formal" sitting meditation at the moment, it's important to pay attention to how you sit. When you sit properly you are firmly planted on the ground and stable. So you want a position that supports you but that is not too uncomfortable or distracting. So to sit stably, you can either sit cross-legged on the floor (on a blanket with a small pillow under your rear end for a little support) or sit on a chair with a straight back. It's important that your posture is good when you sit, so whether you are sitting on the floor or in a chair, your back should be straight. Your posture should be straight and comfortable so you are not slumped down. You should feel that your head is being comfortably held up by your body or almost lifted up. If you are sitting on a chair, your feet should be firmly planted on the ground before (not crossed or anything).

Next relax your shoulders and bring your hands together before you in your lap with your right hand underneath (palm upwards) and your left hand on top of your right hand (palm upwards) forming a little bowl. Then let your thumbs touch each other lightly. This position should be restful and comfortable. If this is too difficult for you, you can start by resting your hands on your thighs, palms either downward or upward.

Now you are ready to meditate.

Meditation techniques
There are many meditation techniques. But here are a few basic ones you can use.

Focus tool no. 5: Focus on the breathing
This is probably the most basic of all meditation techniques. You sit down, get comfortable and then watch your breathing. That's all there is to it. And yes, it sounds easy, but it's difficult to do.

So what happens?

What happens is that you sit and you make the conscious decision to follow your breath. You watch yourself breathe in and breathe out. Why the breath? Because the breath is something we all have and something that is always happening right here, right now.

So you sit and try to follow your breath. After a minute or two, you discover you are off in some thought, absorbed by some fascinating topic like what you forgot to buy at the supermarket or what you saw on TV last night. And when you discover this, you just go back to your breath. You watch your breath again. You breathe and you watch it again. The breath going in and out. You watch what is happening in this moment. Breathing, sitting, this moment. And then you discover you're off again. Lost in another thought. Rehashing what your girlfriend said on the phone today or what your boss said. And then, when you realize what you're doing, you go back to the breath again. Nice and easy. No unkindness here. Don't criticize yourself for being distracted. Don't judge yourself harshly because you find your mind wandering. This is what the mind does, this is what everyone's mind does. Only most of us don't discover this or really realize how distracted we are until we sit down and try to meditate. Then we discover how much our minds wander and how distracted we are. And we see that we are seldom really present and aware of this moment. So just realize when you actually *see* this (when you actually see how distracted you are), it means you are beginning to wake up. Because just this awareness of what your mind is doing is a sign that you are more present than ever before. You are actually present enough to see that your mind wandered off again! (So bravo!)

And this is what meditating on the breath is about. Sitting and seeing what your mind does.

And well that's it.

Sounds simple doesn't it?

Well try it and see!

Counting the breaths

In the beginning, if you find it difficult to stay with the breathing (and you probably will), you can count your breaths for a little while in the beginning—as a kind of crutch. This usually helps. There are different ways to count the breaths, but a simple technique is to say silently to yourself "one" as you breathe in and then "two" as you breathe out, then "three" as you breathe in… and continue until you get to "ten". Then start over again. And if you get distracted and forget to count, well just start over again with "one" when you notice you've lost track. This counting of the breaths will help you settle down in the beginning, but stop counting once you settle down and get used to watching your breathing.

Focus tool no. 6: Focus on a mantra (so-hum)

To help you settle down and focus on the breathing, you can also use the simple "so-hum" mantra to begin with. The "so-hum" mantra is called the mantra of the breath because "so-hum" is like the sound of the air moving in and out of your lungs. If you listen carefully to your breathing, you will see that this is true. So when you meditate and use this mantra, you feel and say the sound "so" silently in your head as you inhale and then you feel and say the sound "hum" silently in your head as you exhale. (Breathe in and out through the nose, not the mouth). It's quite natural and easy to do—and it's very calming because this is the natural sound of your breathing already.

And when you find your mind wandering (which it will do), just come back to the mantra again. Do this for a while until it seems natural for the mantra to disappear into the moment. And then sit and breathe for a while.

Focus tool no. 7: Focus on the witness

Another good basic meditation technique is to focus on the witness. Focusing on the witness means that you focus your attention on who or what it is that is having all the thoughts and experiences you are having. To do this, you can begin like this. First sit quietly and start by focusing for a minute or two on your breathing, just to settle down. Then when you are settled, you can use a minute or two to observe everything you are able to observe in this moment. You can look at your body, you can observe your emotions (what you are feeling), your thoughts, the room around you... briefly go through these things. Then you can ask yourself who or what is observing all this? Who or what is having all these experiences? And this will bring you back to the witnessing Presence, the witnessing consciousness that is naming and experiencing all these things. Then try to observe that. Try to stay with that. Be there. Observe *it, whatever it is*. Experience *it, whatever it is*. Experience this Presence. When you do this, if and when you catch glimpses of this Presence, you are experiencing the witness. Stay with it if you can. And when your mind wanders (which it will probably do), well just go back to the witness when you discover that you have wandered off.

This experience of focusing on the witness, allows you to glimpse your true nature which is non-local, which is the field, the context in which all content (all thoughts and happenings) are unfolding.

And then, when your mind wanders again, just gently return to the witness again, to the observer, which is that which contains all of it. Return to this Presence, return to *whoever* or *whatever* is looking. Look again at the one who distinguishes between the thoughts and the thinker. Look at the one who is perceiving all that you perceive. Look at who or what is observing. And do it again. Keep looking at this observer and you will catch glimpses of the nameless Presence and Power in which all of this so-called life unfolds and which is you! You! The real you! The beingness and the radiance of the Presence behind the world of thoughts and forms.

Reality check: "The seeker is he who is in search of himself

Give up all questions except one: Who am I? After all, the only fact you are sure of is that you are. The 'I am' is certain. The 'I am this' is not. Struggle to find out what you are in reality. To know what you are, you must first investigate and know what you are not.

Discover all that you are not—body, feelings, thoughts, time, space, this or that—nothing concrete or abstract, which you perceive can be you. The very act of perceiving shows that you are not what you perceive. The clearer you understand that on the level of mind you can be described in negative terms only, the quicker will you come to the end of your search and realize that you are the limitless being."

Sri Nisargadatta Maharaj

Context versus content

In connection with observing the witness, it is important to point out here that this book basically contains two different perspectives or ways of looking at our experiences. The one is *content* and the other is *context*.

When we focus on *content*, we are focusing on our daily thoughts and experiences. When we focus on *context*, we are focusing on the consciousness in which all these daily thoughts and experiences arise and disappear.

When we focus on *content*, we can learn how to manage this content (our thoughts) more wisely. This is mind management. And by mind management, I mean learning to understand and use the power of our minds more wisely by learning to focus our attention on the Good we wish to experience. We can also exercise wise mind management by learning to investigate the negative and stressful thinking (thoughts) that are blocking our experience of the goodness of life (see Investigation tools on page 132). In either case—whether we are learning to focus our attention more wisely or whether we are questioning our stressful thinking, we are learning to manage the content of our minds, i.e. our thoughts, more wisely. This is why I call these activities mind management or *content* management. Because we are dealing with our thoughts and all the experiences they engender in us, in other words, we are dealing with the content—which we usually call our life experiences.

But there is another view, the greater view—which is the

context. As we begin to wake up to reality, we begin to see that we can also shift our attention away from *content* to the *context* in which all content is unfolding. In other words, we can withdraw our attention from content, i.e. from our thoughts, words, and actions, and instead focus on the context in which these thoughts and experiences are arising and disappearing. This is what we do, for example, when we focus on the witness in the meditation as just described. Here, we turn our attention away from our thoughts (whatever they are) to the Presence or the Ultimate Reality in which all thoughts and experiences unfold. When we do this, we disregard content, in other words, we disregard our thoughts. We see that thoughts arise, but we do not identify with them or attach to them. We just let them come and go and turn our attention to the context or Presence in which they arise. By doing this, we are focusing on the Presence or Ultimate Reality which is what we are; this is our true nature.

Wise living involves maintaining a good balance between focusing on content and focusing on context. In other words, maintaining a good balance between content management while remembering that our true nature is the context, the real, the Ultimate Reality.

Again wise living is like the two wings of the bird. We need them both to fly harmoniously. In daily life it is the same. We need a good balance between understanding our true nature, which is the eternal Presence beyond all thoughts and experiences, and managing our thoughts and words and actions with clarity and understanding in our daily lives so that we only create that which we truly wish to create. The wise person knows that the law of cause and effect is forever operating in our earthly lives. And thus as we become more wise, we strive to choose the words and actions which are the least harmful and hopefully the most beneficial for ourselves and everyone involved.

That which you are looking with
is what you are looking for.

Focus tool no. 8: Let everything be

Another one of my favorite techniques or triggers when it comes to sitting and being present is to say to myself that now I am not going to resist this moment anymore. Now, for the moment, I am just going to let everything be. I am just going to let everything be as it is. I am not going to resist anything.

It is amazing what this does for me.

Just the thought—*letting everything be*—makes me blissfully happy!

I love it… *just to let everything be.*

I suggest you give it a try.

What happens when you just let everything be as it is? When you have no resistance to anything? When you just are…

How can I describe it?

Why don't you try it for yourself and see what happens.

Why don't you put down this book right now and give it a try.

It's simply so liberating. Also because when you let everything be and rest in this moment, you have no comparisons.

Because what in fact is resistance? Resistance is when you are comparing this moment, this something, to something else. *This* moment can only be "not good enough" if I compare it to something else. Without comparisons, everything is perfectly OK as it is. How could it be otherwise? Without comparisons, I'm home free. Without comparisons there is just this. Just *this*. And what could be wrong with *this* without the thought of *that*? Now you see it don't you? Now you see that without the thought of something else, nothing can possibly be wrong with *this*. Without the thought of "if only", *this is always perfect.* And that's what I always discover when I decide to let everything be.

It's the perfect meditation—always!

Because it's just *this!*

So please give it a try. Just sit and keep coming back to that thought… and let everything be.

Contemplation

One of the best and most scientific ways to lift your consciousness and improve your life is to spend time on a daily basis contemplating the Nature of Reality directly. By dwelling on the qualities of this thing called life, by contemplating the nature of the field itself, you are focusing your attention on the Ultimate Reality which created us all and which sustains and maintains each and every one of us right here, right now. In the old days they sometimes called this type of contemplation *prayer.* Today, great teachers like the Dalai Lama call this kind of contemplation *meditative reflection.* But whatever you call it, considering and dwelling on the eternal verities is a vital and necessary component of your daily practice if you want to make progress and experience the deep inner peace and happiness you seek.

And remember, contemplation always makes you feel better.

Why? Because by contemplating the nature of the field which gave birth to you, you discover that you are a perfect being held in perfect safety in the everlasting arms of eternity—and that there is absolutely nowhere you can fall. And what could be better than this?

So what do you actually do when you contemplate? Well when you contemplate something, firstly you set aside some time—say 15 or 20 minutes—and decide that now you are going to focus your attention on a specific subject. And then you do exactly that. You focus your attention on your selected focal point—for example the nature of the field or the nature of love—and then you consider the subject and mull over it and reflect on the matter from different points of view. You may want to start your contemplation by reading a sacred text which dwells on the subject first to get your mind moving in the right direction. Then you simply sit and dwell on the subject for a while. If you do this on a regular basis, you will discover that pondering or considering a specific subject in this way brings you closer and closer to a deep and lasting experience of whatever you are focusing on.

Focus tool no. 9: Contemplating the Nature of Reality
To contemplate the Nature of Reality, read what follows slowly and then sit and think about all of this for a while.

All the most advanced thinkers and awakened ones throughout the history of our planet have agreed that there is ONE Power, Force, Presence, Deity or Supreme Being behind all of creation. This Ultimate Reality is often called God, the Supreme Being, the Creator, the Higher Power, the Almighty, the Presence, Allah, Brahman and various other names in various other times and cultures; but whatever people choose to call this ONE Presence or Power, It is the Cause of all creation; It is all of creation.

To simplify matters, let us call the animating Force behind all of creation the "ONE". Now let these words and thoughts fill your mind.

We can deduce and recognize that since this ONE created all there is, this ONE must also be all there is. In other words, this ONE must be all of existence — or "Life" itself. And since nothing else exists but this ONE, this ONE must therefore also be all of It — all of creation.

From this we can conclude that since this ONE is the only Life there is, It must be everywhere, and in everything and in everyone. So this ONE, which many people call God, the Presence, the Ultimate Reality is the animating Force behind all of creation. In other words, this ONE is the First Cause, i.e., the Cause and Originator of all creation. Further back than this we cannot go.

The ONE

Now since this ONE is the First Cause and Originator and all there is; it means there is no opposing force. There is nothing in existence but this ONE. This is extremely important to understand—and all further realization is based on understanding this concept. So I repeat: *Since there is only ONE First Cause and Originator, only ONE Life and ONE animating force or Presence, it means there is no opposing force.* If there were an opposing force, it would mean that there are two forces.

In the world of physical manifestation, this idea of ONE is also confirmed by quantum physics and the theory of the unified field. According to the latest scientific research, all of manifest creation is one vast field of energy. Physicists say that the atoms that make up you, me and everything else in our world are all identical and interchangeable. And that these identical and interchangeable atoms are made up of the same identical and interchangeable sub-atomic particles which all can be broken down into waves of energy. These waves of energy are what form the one interconnected unified field that is all of manifest creation and that gives rise to all of manifest creation.

So let us explore some of the characteristics of this ONE unified field of energy which we are now calling the ONE Life because It is all that exists.

All-powerful: Since the ONE is all there is, then this ONE Life must be all-powerful. In other words, when there is only ONE, there is no opposing force. So there is nothing to resist the ONE. So It—the ONE Life—is all power.

All-present: Since the ONE Life is all there is, It must be everywhere or all-present. In other words, It must be fully present throughout all of creation. Ergo, It must also be the same ONE Life that is animating all of creation, including you, me and everyone and everything else.

All-knowing: The ONE, which is all there is and which is what we are, is aware. We know this because we are aware. We are conscious beings; we know and thus we can see that we are this consciousness, this awareness. This is what we are. We are It, the ONE Life, being aware of Itself through us. We are this knowingness, this awareness. We are the Infinite Mind of the ONE Life, which is all there is.

Thus we see that Infinite Mind is the all-knowing intelligence of the ONE Life since It conceived of, created, and contains all of creation. What could be more intelligent than this? What can know more than all of creation? What could be more intelligent than the intelligence that created the dazzling dance of creation which is beyond our wildest fantasy? This intelligence, which created the vastness of space with its myriad galaxies, the intricacies of our bodies, and the breathtaking web of all Life that extends from dimension to dimension, is what we are. We are this Infinite Mind, the Mind which contains all of it. That is our true nature.

Thus we see there can be no intelligence which It does not contain since It is all of It. Thus, nothing you, I or anyone else can conceive of can be inconceivable for the ONE Life, the ONE Mind, since we are all living, moving, thinking and breathing within this ONE Life.

Truth: Truth is what is. Truth is that which never changes. So the ONE Life or existence must be the Truth because the ONE Life is all there is. In fact, Life or existence is the only thing we know for sure. We know that Life is because we are. We exist. In other words, you know that Life is because you exist. You could say that you are proof of your own existence. (Can you remember a time when you didn't exist?) So this must be Truth. Ergo you are Truth. Life and Truth are one and the same. And that's what you are—Life and Truth.

Peace and harmony: Another characteristic of the ONE Life must be harmony. This is because there is only ONE. ONE Life, ONE field, ONE Mind, ONE consciousness. As we said before, when you have only ONE, it means there is no opposing or conflicting force. When there is no opposing force, there is no discord—no disharmony. So the ONE Life is another word for peace and harmony.

Love: Peace and harmony—or lack of disharmony or conflict—is also a way of describing Love, the harmonizing factor. (We all know that fear is the opposite of Love. It is interesting to note that the Sanskrit word for fear is two.) And since the ONE is all there is, it means It must be perfectly safe and at home with Itself. What could be safer and more at home than being the ONE Life which is all of It? And that is what we are. Thus we see that the ONE Life, which is us, is the ultimate safety and support, always holding us in Its everlasting arms. Embracing everything and everyone unconditionally now and throughout eternity.

Infinite: Science tells us that the unified field or the ONE Life is infinite. Infinite means without beginning or end, so the ONE Life must go on unto infinity.

Abundance: Since the ONE Life, the ONE unified field is all there is, all of creation is contained within It. All of creation is another word for the infinite abundance that manifests everything out of itself, the unified field.

Indestructible: Another characteristic of the ONE Life is that it is indestructible. Even science tells us that nothing can be destroyed, things only change form. So we know that the ONE Life goes on forever and ever, changing form and changing form again and again until infinity but never disappearing. And since there is no opposing force, nothing can harm or destroy this field, which is what we are—you and me.

Eternal: Since the unified field or ONE Life is indestructible, it must also be eternal. In other words, it goes on forever. Without beginning or end—and this means you and me. In this connection ask yourself—can you remember a time when you did not exist?

Immortal: Eternal is another way of saying immortal which means that the ONE Life never dies. And since It never dies, we know this means It was never born either.

Principle: Since the ONE Life is eternal and immortal—and without beginning or end—we can see that the ONE Life must be principle or law. Because as we ascertained at the beginning of this book, a law or principle is something that never changes and is always true. And since this ONE Life is eternal and immortal, it never changes and is always true. Thus this ONE Life is unchanging law or principle.

Perfect Good: From all this we can deduce that since this ONE Life is all that exists, it must be the unchanging Principle of Perfect Good. Why Good? Well what is your definition of Good? What is Good? Your definition, your highest definition of Good, is the same as everyone else's highest definition of Good. The Good that you seek—the Good that everyone seeks—is unlimited Life, unlimited Love, unlimited Peace and Harmony, unlimited Abundance. And, as we have just seen, all of these definitions of Good are the characteristics of the ONE Life—of the one unified field. Therefore we know that the ONE Life is the unchanging Principle of Perfect Good! And this is what you are!

Contemplate these ideas over and over again

Now these are just some ideas—some statements of truth—you can use when you want to contemplate the Nature of Reality. This type of thinking is vitally important when it comes to transforming your life as I said at the beginning of this section.

Now why is that so? Because as we now know, all thought is creative and because your thoughts and underlying beliefs are creating your experience of reality, your experience of this thing we call life. And this means that when you contemplate the ideas and statements of truth outlined above, you are bringing your thoughts and underlying beliefs closer to the truth and more into alignment with the Ultimate Reality. You are harmonizing your thinking with the nature of the ONE Life and turning your focus away from any old, incorrect and limiting ideas you may have had about this thing called life. In other words, you are turning away from your old limiting patterns of thought and replacing these thoughts with powerful thoughts of truth instead (See the Law of Substitution, page 73).

This change of focus can and will change your life because what you focus your attention on grows in your experience. So by aligning your thoughts with the all-powerful ONE Life, which we know is unlimited intelligence, unlimited Life, unlimited Love, unlimited peace, unlimited harmony, unlimited abundance, in short—unlimited Good—you will begin to experience more and more of these qualities in your daily life.

This is the incredible power of contemplation. And the secret behind the incredible power of contemplation is this—*whatever you focus your attention on grows.*

Other good texts to contemplate

There are many good texts you can use for contemplation. Here are some of my favorites. To use these texts—or any others you may prefer—read the chosen section either silently or out loud and then sit quietly and contemplate these words of wisdom for 10-15 minutes.

- Deepak Chopra's description of the 25 qualities of the unified field from Chapter 4 of his book "Creating Affluence".
- Emmet Fox's description of the One Presence in the section called "The Presence" at the end of his book "Power through Constructive Thinking".
- The end of the second chapter of the "Bhagavad Gita" which ends with Krishna describing the high state of consciousness that leads to liberation.
- The psalm "The Lord is My Shepherd".
- Any of the sayings of the Buddha in "The Dhammapada", starting with Chapter 1.

The Golden Key

In his piece "The Golden Key", the great spiritual teacher Emmet Fox says quite simply that the fastest and most effective way to deal with any type of trouble is to: "*Stop thinking about the difficulty, whatever it is, and think about God instead.* This is the complete rule, and if only you will do this, the trouble, whatever it is, will presently disappear. It makes no difference what kind of trouble it is. It may be a big thing or a little thing; it may concern health, finance, a law-suit, a quarrel, an accident, or anything else conceivable; but whatever it is, just stop thinking about it, and think of God instead — that is all you have to do."

This approach is recommended by almost every great spiritual teacher who has walked this earth. Lift your consciousness and the trouble will disappear. And lifting your consciousness means thinking about the great verities, meditating on the great verities. It means turning your attention to the ONE Life which is all of It. Lifting your consciousness means turning your focus away from your problems, whatever they are. And then focusing on the Absolute; focusing on the Nature of Reality. It means meditating on *God is All and God is Good.*

All the Great Ones point to the power of focus. Jesus said, "If therefore thine eye be single, thy whole body shall be full of light" (Matthew 6:22). Mary Baker Eddy said, "Stand porter at the door of thought." And the prophet Isaiah said, "Look unto me, and be ye saved, all the ends of the earth: for I *am* God, and *there is* none else." (Isaiah 45:22)

Next time you face a serious difficulty, lift your consciousness by switching your attention to the great verities. Focus on a sacred text such as the psalm "The Lord is My Shepherd". Read it over and over again. Repeat it slowly in your mind. Dwell on each sentence and the meaning of each phrase. Let the power of this sacred text fill your mind and heart. And see what happens. This is the Golden Key to harmony and happiness that Emmet

Fox is talking about.

Focus tool no. 10: Contemplating love

Another good focal point for contemplation is love. Dwelling regularly on love can work wonders in your life—whether it be in your relationships, on the job, or in your health. Love in all its aspects always bestows comfort, peace and healing, especially when you focus on the unconditional love and support of Life itself and build a sense of universal good will in yourself towards all of humankind.

To contemplate love, you can start by reading one of your favorite passages about love to help you get your thoughts moving in the right direction. Sit quietly and read the text of your choice slowly. You can read it out loud or silently, whatever suits you best. Once you've read the text carefully considering what it says, turn these ideas over in your mind for a while, savoring them and making them a part of your life. This is not just an intellectual exercise so allow yourself to feel the love in your own heart.

To inspire you, here are two of my favorite passages. The first is by Emmet Fox from the chapter entitled "The Golden Gate" from the final section of his book "Power Through Constructive Thinking":

"There is no difficulty that enough love will not conquer; no disease that enough love will not heal; no door that enough love will not open; no gulf that enough love will not bridge; no wall that enough love will not throw down; no sin that enough love will not redeem.

It makes no difference how deeply seated may be the trouble, how hopeless the outlook, how muddled the tangle, how great the mistake; a sufficient realization of love will dissolve it. If only you could love enough you would be the happiest and most powerful being in the world."

I just love this text and love to dwell on it.

Here is another good one:

"I Corinthians, Chapter 13

THOUGH I speak with the tongues of men and angels, and have not love, I am become as sounding brass or a tinkling cymbal.

2 And though I have the gift of prophecy, and understand all mysteries, and all knowledge: and though I have all faith so that I could remove mountains, and have not love, I am nothing.

3 And though I bestow all my goods to feed the poor, and though I give my body to be burned, and have not love, it profiteth me nothing.

4. Love suffereth long, and is kind: love envieth not: love vaunnteth not itself, is not puffed up,

5 Doth not behave itself unseemly, seeketh not her own, is not easily provoked, thinketh no evil;

6 Rejoiceth not in iniquity, but rejoiceth in truth;

7 Beareth all things, believeth all things, hopeth all things, endureth all things.

8 Love never faileth: but whether there be prophecies, they shall fail; whether there be tongues, they shall cease; whether there be knowledge, it shall vanish away.

9 For we know in part, and we prophesy in part.

10 But when that which is perfect is come, then that which is in part shall be done away.

11 When I was a child, I spake as a child, I understood as a child, I thought as a child: but when I became a man, I put away childish things.

12 For now we see through a glass, darkly; but then face to face: now I know in part; but then shall I know even as also I am known.

13 And now abideth faith, hope, love, these three; but the greatest of them is love."

Focus tool no. 11: Mental treatment or scientific prayer

Mental treatment or scientific prayer is another powerful form of contemplation.

Mental treatment is a specific, directed movement of mind — of your mind — in which you work with your thoughts until they are in alignment with the Nature of Reality. Mental treatment, which is sometimes called scientific prayer, is another good way of using the power of your mind to focus on the truth about your life and your situation. The difference between general contemplation and mental treatment is that in mental treatment you move your focus from contemplation of universal truths and principles to focus on the specific—either your own life or another person's—or on a specific situation.

When you do a mental treatment for yourself for example, you move from contemplating the universal characteristics of the ONE Life to seeing these very same characteristics in your own life. What you are actually doing is systematically explaining to yourself that whatever is true of the whole—of the ONE universal Life—must also be true of you, since you live and breathe and move and have your being within this ONE Life and are in fact this ONE Life. So when treating in this way, you are actually convincing yourself that everything that is true of the ONE Life is also true of your own individual life. When you have succeeded in establishing this fact (in convincing yourself)—that everything that is true of the ONE Life is also true of you and your life, your treatment is complete.

We often call this stage—getting your realization. We say this because this is when you actually get the sense or feeling that yes, everything that is true of the ONE Life really is true of my life. This is your realization. When this happens, when you feel satisfied that this is the truth about you, your work is done. So just sit quietly for a few moments and give thanks. Then go about your daily business. If during the day, any thoughts arise that contradict your treatment, just remind yourself briefly of your treatment. You can repeat your treatment several times a day if it feels right to you, especially if you are in a challenging situation. And then see what happens!

Here is a sample treatment for health and harmony in your life and your affairs now. You can do this treatment by either reading it slowly out loud or by saying it slowly and silently in your head. If the treatment is for you—use your own name just as I use my name below. If you are doing this treatment for someone else, use the other person's name instead of your own.

This treatment is for me, Barbara Berger. The words that I speak are the truth about me, Barbara Berger, and they go forth into the Great Universal Mind and they do not return unto me void. But they accomplish the things of which I speak with mathematical precision.

There is only ONE Life and that Life is Perfect, Perfect Good, Perfect Love, Perfect Harmony—and that Life is my life now. And I know that this ONE Perfect Life, which is All Power, All Presence, All Knowledge and All Love, created me and is now sustaining and maintaining me in Perfect Harmony with All that is.

And I give thanks for this ONE Life, I trust in It, I surrender to It, I am amazed by It, I am grateful for It... because I know that the ONE Life's Perfect Plan for me is unfolding now and that this Perfect Plan is everlasting Life and Perfect Balance and Harmony in my mind, body and all my affairs now.

I also give thanks because I now that the ONE Life, which is Perfect Divine Love, is the only Power operating in my life right now. And since It is the only power, there is nothing to oppose or resist it. So I rest and relax in the Love of this ONE Perfect Life and watch as the ONE Perfect Life and ONE Perfect Love works in and through me right now. Guiding and directing my life and all my affairs now. Showing me exactly what to do. Healing and comforting, uplifting and inspiring, balancing and relaxing. Harmonizing everything in my mind, body and affairs now.

Because this is the truth, I know this means there is no disharmony, no tension, no blockages, no lack of supply, no pain, no disease, nor lack of Life anywhere in me because I am the Perfect Child of this ONE Perfect Life.

Everything I do reflects the Goodness and perfection of the ONE Perfect Life that is working in and through me. This means that I am

Love in action. This means that everything I think, say and do is Love in action. I am a living demonstration of the Goodness of the ONE Perfect Life.

Knowing this, I rest and relax in the Love of the ONE Perfect Life and know that this Love, this Goodness is working in and through me for the Highest Good of All Concerned now.

I thank the Great Universal Power, the ONE Life, for all the Good in my life now.

And so it is!

A short, effective treatment

Here is a short, but very effective treatment or scientific prayer from Tim's novels "Starbrow" and "Starwarrior". It's the condensed version of the longer treatments outlined above and it's a good one to have in your pocket to bring out when in need. A quick and excellent way to remind yourself of the Nature of Reality. Say it out loud or silently in your head, one or more times. Instead of using the word "Good", you can use another word or aspect of the Nature of Reality such as: "Divine Love", "Peace", "Divine Wisdom" or "Perfect Life".

"In the Beginning: The Good
Here and Now: The Good
At the End of the End: The Good
Here, There, Everywhere: The Good
From Alpha to Omega: The Good
In Heaven, upon Earth: The Good
In the Greatest, in the Smallest: The Good
In Fire, in Water, in Earth, in Air: The Good
In Me, in You, in Everyone: The Good
Above Me, below Me, around Me: The Good
In Me, through Me, from Me: The Good
In My Thoughts, in My Words, in My Actions: The Good
The Good is All in All

All Life, All Intelligence, All Love
The Good is the One and Only Reality
And So It Is!"

For more ideas for treatments, see my other books or the books of Ernest Holmes, Emmet Fox, Emma Curtis Hopkins and Catherine Ponder. Or make your own treatment.

INVESTIGATION TOOLS

In this section, we are going to explore what I call "investigation tools" which are techniques that can help us identify, question, and lessen our attachment to the negative thoughts and beliefs that are preventing us from experiencing the goodness of life which is fully present right now. Learning to do this is vitally important because when we learn to question our stressful thinking and the negative programming we have all received, we are on the road to uncovering and experiencing the happiness we seek.

Now why do I say this?

Well if we go back to our original exploration, let us remind ourselves once again that we now are beginning to see more and more clearly that all our experiences are just thoughts in our minds. We are learning to recognize that there is *reality*, the real, *this*, whatever is happening now, and then there are our thoughts about *this*—whatever *this is*—that is happening right now. And that's all that's going on.

The reality is we are here now and stuff is happening. That's reality. We only get into trouble (experience unhappiness or suffer) when we resist what is happening by telling ourselves that things should be different from the way they are, in other words, when we say to "no" to this moment. When we do this, when we say "no" to reality, we create stress and misery for ourselves. Because remember, reality is what it is. This moment is what it is. We don't have a say in the matter, we don't have a choice. Life does what it does. That's all there is to it. Both inner and outer events are just that—they are events. They are the things that happen. In and of themselves, they have no intrinsic value. It is our interpretations of these inner and outer events that make us feel good or bad, happy or sad.

When you understand this, you are waking up to reality! You are "getting real" as we often call our work.

This is what waking up to reality is all about.

Waking up is seeing that there is reality and then there is our interpretation of what is going on—and being very clear about the fact that there is probably a big difference between the two, especially if you are unhappy! So waking up to reality is seeing clearly that when these two things don't match, we suffer. That's what suffering is. Suffering is when our thinking and reality don't match. Suffering is when we think life "should" be different than it is. Suffering arises when we think people "should" be different from what they are. Suffering arises when we think we "should" be different than we are.

And again I would like to point out we're not talking about right or wrong here or what's fair or unfair. We're talking about reality. We're talking about the fact that life does what it does. But this is not to say you cannot live sensibly and work for a better world and improve your life. What I am talking about is the reality of *this moment. This* moment is what it is. Nothing you can do can change this. This moment is already done.

And it's the constant battle against *this moment* that wears us out and makes us miserable. It's the constant battle against *this moment* that robs us of our peace of mind and of the deep inner happiness that is our true nature. And no one's doing this to us... we're doing it to ourselves! Quite innocently of course. Because most of us are unaware of what we are doing. We're unaware of the mechanism. We're unconscious; we're asleep. We don't see how our minds work, which is why I say, if you want to live a happy life, it's time to wake up! It's now or never! Your happy life is right here, right now. The peace of mind you seek is right here, right now.

Unfortunately, for most of us it's quite another story. For most of us, when things happen, we automatically click into our old stories, dire predictions based on past programming, and beliefs about what life "should" be that we've never questioned. And when we do this, this is where the fight with reality begins—and all the unhappiness, suffering and anguish that goes with it.

I have come to see that we're all drama queens and experts (me included) when it comes to indulging in "catastrophic" thinking when in reality nothing whatsoever is going on. And by catastrophic thinking, I mean the thousand and one ingenious ways in which we regularly and relentlessly scare ourselves to death. It's quite amazing—and we're doing it all the time! When you start to get a little insight into the mechanism, you will discover that you are a master at taking the most innocent situation and making it into a full-blown drama or crisis situation. And we do it all the time. You lose your keys and it's the end of the world. Your boyfriend forgets to call and you're sure he's in bed with another woman. You have a stomach ache and you're on death row. You lose your job and you see yourself wandering the street as a homeless bag lady. Who needs television when each one of us has our own private fear machine (our very own CNN) inside our heads!

But reality, oh reality, the simplicity of what is before us... do we ever notice that?

Noticing the real

So what happens when you actually decide to do this—to notice reality? What happens when you say to yourself, OK, I'm going to drop all my thoughts about the meaning of what's going on right now and just be present here and notice reality. What do you have then? What happens? (And again I'm not talking about right and wrong here, I'm just talking about what is actually going on in front of you.)

When I try this exercise, when I say to myself, I'm just going to be present with no thoughts about what all this means, the first thing I always notice is that suddenly it gets very peaceful. And there is a spaciousness about everything and an ease to being. There is also a delightful softness and a sense of ease about *this moment* because my resistance is gone. I've said "yes" to this moment. I've stopped fighting what is and I am allowing it to unfold. And everything does unfold, all by itself. And I need do nothing, or should we say, I can do nothing. It's all very simple. Everything is being "done" for me.

Another thing I often notice when I stop resisting is this powerful feeling of Presence. The powerful feeling of the *suchness* of *this*, of being alive, of life itself. It's as if a hidden radiance shines forth... or perhaps it's just that I actually notice it! The fullness and utter simplicity of *this* moment whatever it is. Sitting here at my computer. The light coming in through the window. The clock ticking on the wall. The sun going down. The flowers in the vase next to me.

It's very peaceful. (I'm very peaceful).

Life is.

All the complications were only in my head.

So it's worth trying, it's worth going to this place beyond thoughts, because when we drop our stories and expectations and our interpretations of events, we find a peace that passes all human understanding, a peace that was always present but which we never noticed because we were so occupied with our stories that we didn't notice reality. We forgot (or we never learned or experienced) that reality is ours, always and that it's right here and much simpler than anything we can possibly imagine.

When you find this place, it might seem like magic because it's so amazing and wonderful, but the truth is it's been here all along. The truth is, it was just you driving yourself crazy while beautiful life was unfolding all around you all the time.

So this is why this section is about investigating the stories, beliefs and expectations that are preventing us from experiencing the beautiful reality that is right in front of our eyes.

Take my word for it—it's something you don't want to miss!

Reality check: Unconditional happiness

When I use the word "happiness" in this book, I am talking about unconditional happiness, the happiness that is totally independent of outer conditions and circumstances, the happiness that is not dependent on other people. This is what I mean by unconditional happiness. Unconditional happiness is the happiness that no job, no amount of money in the bank, no lover, no guru, no success or amount of fame can bring you. When you are happy because of other people or because of outside circumstances, conditions or events—your happiness is conditional because it is based on these people or events living up to your value judgments, belief systems, and stories. Not that there is anything wrong with conditional happiness, but it is important to realize that when our happiness is conditional, sooner or later it will disappear because it is dependent on and triggered by external events, circumstances and other people which can, will and do change.

The happiness you experience in the present moment for no particular reason when you are mindful is your true nature. It's unconditional because it depends on no one or thing. It's who you are.

Investigation tool no. 1: No comparisons (a meditation or contemplation)

Here is a wonderful pointer to help you see reality.

Ask yourself who would you be if you couldn't compare this moment with any other moment? Ask yourself, how would this moment be if you couldn't compare this moment to any other moment?

How would it be if this instance in time, right now, stood all alone, all by itself and you simply couldn't compare *this* to anything else? How would *this* be? How would *this* feel? Now please just bear with me for a moment and don't laugh (OK laugh but bear with me anyway) because it's a very interesting experiment.

So let's go there.

Let's go to *this moment with no comparisons.*

This moment.

How would it be if now was all you had? How would it be if you couldn't remember? If this moment was all you knew? Please allow yourself to go there just as an experiment. Because, trust me, it's an interesting one. Because who would you be — and what would this moment be — without memory? Just let yourself go there for a moment.

What am I driving at?

I'm driving at the fact that if we couldn't compare this moment to any other moment — this moment would be absolutely perfect. And I repeat — absolutely perfect — no matter what is happening.

Just think about it. If you couldn't compare *this* to anything else — what could possibly be "wrong" with *this*?

Now you see it, don't you?

Now you see that "wrong" is always a comparison.

Wrong is always a relative position in relation to something else.

"This" or anything else can only be "wrong" compared to *"that"* or something else. The thought that "this moment should be different than it is" can only arise in comparison to some other moment. *This* in itself cannot be "wrong". *This* in itself just is. And actually *just is* is all there is. The rest — all the comparisons — are just thoughts in our minds. They are not reality, which is a very important fact to keep in mind. Reality is *this*. Period. Full

stop. Nothing else is reality.

I know this is very hard to grasp, but it's true nevertheless. There is nothing else but now. We may believe there is a past and a future, but there isn't. There never was—and there never will be. Past and future are just stories we have, which of course are quite OK. But when the stories become so real (in our imaginations) that we miss *this* or think (and experience) *this* as "wrong"—then perhaps it's time to reconsider and take another look. Especially if the "wrong" thought makes us suffer, sick, unhappy, tense...

So if you can, just allow yourself to be present without comparing this moment to anything else and see what happens.

I have also discovered that this is an excellent way to enter into any experience that you think is going to be difficult or challenging. If you decide in advance to go into the experience without comparisons, you might be very surprised at what happens. I know I always am!

Psychological versus practical time

Oh but you say, we have to comparisons because we are living in time and space. So what about time? Don't we need time? And the answer is yes, time is a very useful concept for functioning in this world and so is memory. Time and memory help us function in the most practical sense of the word. Obviously you don't want to have to learn how to make coffee each and every morning when you go out to the kitchen! But in this connection, it's important to see how we are using the concept of time.

In his masterpiece "The Power of Now", Eckhart Tolle talks about two types of time, "clock time" and "psychological time"—and I think his distinctions are very relevant. Practical or clock time (as he calls it) is what we are all using when we buy airplane tickets or learn something or schedule appointments or go to work in the morning. Clock time is obviously a practical way of planning and using time which we all need. The problem with time arises when we get stuck in what Tolle calls psychological time. And by psychological time he is referring to the time we use reminiscing, rehashing and dwelling on the past or projecting and worrying about the future. When we use time like this, we move away from reality—and this usually makes us suffer.

So it can be very useful to start noticing how you are using time. Are you using it practically to function in the world—or are you spending a lot of mental energy in the past and future? If you find yourself doing this, it's up to you to bring yourself back to this moment—and stop comparing "this" to "that".

Our stories

But you say, it's not just about the ability to be present in this moment, it's also about all the beliefs and stories that prevent us from being present and happy now. And yes, this is true too. Because if you look at what you are doing, you will see that it is true that we bring so many beliefs and stories to the present moment that we cannot see the trees (*this moment*) for the forest (our stories). We are so identified with the stories that we believe they are reality. And so we miss what is.

When we start to see this, we discover that the stories we have that are covering up the beauty of *this moment* can range from anything which concerns our health and well-being to our stories about our relationships, finances and the future. When you see what you're doing, you discover it's a zoo. There are so many stories going on in our heads all the time! But precisely what stories am I talking about? I'm talking about the stories we all have because no one is special in this respect. We all have pretty much the same stories going on in our heads, so even if each of us has our own personal spin on the stories, we're all in the same boat. Obviously, we were all brought up hearing the same stories! There might be variations on our major themes, but we're all basically telling ourselves the same things.

One of our main story lines is about our bodies and our health. Most of us worry about life in these physical bodies and about the maintenance and upkeep of life in these bodies. And we have the most brilliant stories (and scenarios) when it comes to scaring ourselves. Not only do we worry about how we look and feel, we tell ourselves stories about what every ache and pain might mean. (Yes we're all experts at catastrophic thinking!) And then as we get older, we worry about getting old and not being able to take care of ourselves. And we worry about dying. Did you ever meet anyone who doesn't? Well I haven't, though I have heard of a few wise souls who aren't so identified with their stories—and their bodies—anymore. But in general, I think it's fair to say that most of us do have a lot of stories (many of them very scary) about these bodies. Don't you? And what about your friends? Aren't they worried about the same things as you are? And what about your parents and family? Aren't they worried about the same things as you are? When you look closely, I think you will discover that most of us have pretty much the same stories and fears and that most of our stories and fears are connected to our bodies. Because without a body, what could we worry about? Even our stories (and worries) about money and survival are because of our bodies. I mean could you worry about the rent if you didn't have a body to take care of?

Here are some of the thoughts that pop up in almost everyone's head:

- If I get sick, I won't be able to manage.
- My body should be well and strong (even if it isn't).
- If something happens to my body, I won't be able to function.
- Life is dangerous.
- The world is a scary place.
- There is something wrong with me.
- I am not OK.

- Life isn't fair.
- I won't be able to take care of myself.
- I'll end up all alone.
- Something bad will happen to me and I'll be dependent on others.
- If my partner leaves, I won't be able to manage.
- Being sick is dangerous.
- Pain is awful.
- Pain is unfair.
- I need insurance because something might go wrong.
- I need money in the bank because something might go wrong.
- I need security.
- I need to protect myself.
- And so on...

Be honest with yourself—haven't you had these very thoughts from time to time?

The underworld of beliefs
The thoughts listed above are just a small selection of the underworld of thoughts and beliefs most of us have. And these thoughts and beliefs pop up regularly (for many of us) and really make us suffer.

There's another interesting thing going on here I'd like to mention. In connection with this underworld of thoughts and beliefs, I have noticed that even if you are diligently working with the focus tools described in the previous section of this book and are focusing on the goodness of reality, if your underlying stories and beliefs are very fearful and scary, they will often block your experience of the goodness of life. I know this has been my experience because even though I used focus tools for years, I didn't know how to deal with the stories and beliefs I had which were scaring me.

Let's take an example. Let's say you are working with the focus tool called "Notice the support" described on page 103. And you spend time every day noticing the support of life all around you. This is of course a wonderful thing to do—to train yourself to be mindful of the support of life. And the more you notice this and focus on this, the more it becomes your experience. But here's the problem: What if—at the same time as you are focusing on the support—you really believe deep in your heart (in other words this is your story) that life doesn't support you? What if you go around noticing the support while you have the firm belief that this is not true—that life doesn't support you? What if you believe you're all alone in a cold, lonely universe that doesn't care about you? If this is the case, obviously it will be difficult for you to truly relax and experience the support of life, even if you are focusing all your attention on this support.

Are focus tools enough?

So this is a most important question to consider. Is it enough to focus on the good we want to experience? Perhaps for some people it is, but I have noticed that many people who are working diligently with focus tools still are not experiencing the happiness and peace of mind they are seeking. Having seen this, I have come to believe that this is because focus tools alone are not enough for these people. Focus tools might seem to be enough for a while (and they are of course a great place to start working with your mind), but in my experience, if we haven't dealt with the underlying beliefs and stories that are scaring us and making us unhappy and fearful, focus tools by themselves are not enough to really set us free.

So this is why I say investigating our stressful thoughts and scary stories, is so important. Investigating our thinking is what I call the other wing of the bird. The one wing of the bird is focus tools and the other wing is investigation tools. And to fly happily through life, I believe a combination of focus tools and investigation tools works best.

So how do we investigate our stories?

So if a combination of focus tools and investigation tools is best, the question is how do we actually do this? How do we actually identify the specific thoughts and stories that are bothering us and how do we investigate them?

Well of course there are many ways.

If you think you have a brain tumor or cancer or heart trouble, you can go to your doctor and get a check-up. Then you'll know whether it's true or not. If it's true then you can take it from there. And if it's not, well then you can forget about it and stop worrying. And the same goes for all the other scary stories we have about life. If you are having problems with your partner or at work, you can, for example, go to a psychologist or a therapist and tell your stories, and he or she will help you find out how much of what you are saying it true—and then you can work with that. Cognitive behavioral therapy, for example, seeks to help people test their beliefs and assumptions and identify the unquestioned thoughts they have which are distorted, unrealistic and over-generalizations. By doing this, people can develop a more realistic (and kinder) approach to their lives and problems. And of course, you can also talk to your friends, because friends usually want to hear our stories (that's why they are our friends). But this of course can be dangerous, especially if your friends always agree with you! The best friends are the ones who question your stories, especially if they are causing you distress.

But by far the best modern-day tool I know to investigate our thoughts, stories and beliefs is "The Work of Byron Katie".

The Work of Byron Katie

The Work of Byron Katie consists of four simple questions and a turnaround that anyone can use to examine their fears, worries and stories and see if they are true or not. The Work is a modern-day version of the traditional inquiry techniques and is definitely for people who are on the fast track. If you want to know the truth, do "The Work" because like so many of our teachers have said, only the truth can set us free. Most of us agree with this observation, but the trouble is, most of us don't really know how to do this in practice. We don't know how to find the truth. And up until now, we didn't have a simple technique we could use to identify what is true and what is not. But I believe Byron Katie's four questions are the tool we've been looking for. The questions are so simple that anyone can use them. And they are effective because they cut through to the heart of the matter quickly and easily. And you don't need to go to a therapist to ask the questions nor do you need special training to use them by yourself. All you have to do is sit down quietly (either by yourself or with a friend or partner) write down the thoughts and beliefs that are bothering you, and then ask the four questions and turn your statements around. And see what happens.

Byron Katie's four questions are:
"1. Is it true?
2. Can you absolutely know that it's true?
3. How do you react when you think that thought?
4. Who would you be without the thought?
and
The turnaround (the exact opposite of the original statement)"

From Byron Katie's book "Loving What Is". For a detailed description of how to do "The Work" read this book or check out her Web site www.thework.com.

In my experience, when I do "The Work" and ask the four questions, so many of my fears and worries just dissolve and disappear. And all I did was write down the thoughts that are bothering me and ask the questions. I didn't make any special effort at all, it's really rather uncanny how it works. When I find my own truth and discover that something I was so afraid of is simply not true, it dissolves and then slowly fades from my life. And it's not because I am trying to make the belief go away. It's more because when I shine the light of truth on the belief or thought, I often find it just doesn't hold water. And then I begin to see reality. I begin to see what's really going on. I begin to see the real, instead of being blinded by my story about life. And then what happens? Well then the fear or worry diminishes (and sometimes even fades away) and then the radiance of my real life—*this life*—really does shine forth right now! I admit sometimes it seems like a miracle is taking place. I don't try to stop worrying about something, when I investigate the fear thought, I just *do* stop worrying.

But I also have to admit, this doesn't happen overnight. In my experience this too is something we have to "work" at because we have so many stories and worries that are bothering us. So today doing "The Work" has become a regular part of my daily practice. I have discovered that when I work with thoughts that are bothering me in one area of my life and get a little clearer, then another area pops up and calls for my attention. So the process continues and each time I do "The Work", I find I am able to go deeper. And each time I end up feeling a little bit clearer and a little bit saner than I was before! It's really truly lovely! And liberating!

Investigation tool no. 2: Doing "The Work"

To help you get a clearer idea of the process, let's take an example and do "The Work" on it. Let's do "The Work" on the thought we mentioned above—on the thought *"Life doesn't support me."*

Question: So Barbara, *life doesn't support you.* Is that true?

(Question 1)

Barbara: Yes. Life is a struggle and I have to work so hard to take care of myself and achieve anything. (These are good sub-thoughts to investigate after doing the Work on the original thought ... "I have to work so hard to take care of myself." "I have to work so hard to achieve anything.")

Question: So Barbara is it true that *life doesn't support you*? Can you absolutely know that it's true that *life doesn't support you*? What is the reality? Are you here now? Are you breathing? Is your body functioning? Is the world here? The earth, the trees, the sky? Is there food in your refrigerator? Do you have money in the bank? What's the reality Barbara? Is life supporting you?

Barbara: Well yes.

Question: So can you absolutely know that it's true that *life is not supporting you*? (Question 2).

Barbara: No.

Question: OK Barbara, so how does it make you feel when you believe this thought that *life is not supporting you?* (Question 3).

Barbara: It makes me feel scared and lonely, like I'm all alone in a cold world and no one will take care of me. It makes me feel I have to do it all by myself. It makes me feel that life is dangerous. (Another good thought to investigate—"Life is dangerous.")

Question: That sounds rather stressful.

Barbara: Yes, it really is.

Question: So believing this thought that *life does not support you*—which you just said you could not absolutely know is true—does this thought bring peace into your life or what?

Barbara: No, it's a horrible thought. It makes me feel terrible. Afraid and lonely.

Question: So who would you be Barbara without the thought *life does not support you?* (Question 4). Who would you be if you simply could not believe this thought?

Barbara: I'd be so much more relaxed and happy in the world. I'd feel so much safer and better about life.

Question: And how would you live your life without this thought?

Barbara: Actually I think I would have a lot more fun.

Question: That sounds like a nice way to live. So now let's turn the thought around. What is the exact opposite of your original statement? (The turnaround).

Barbara: *Life does support me.*

Question: Could that be as true as or truer than your original statement?

Barbara: Yes it could.

Question: So give me three specific examples of how life is supporting you.

Barbara: Well, I do have this body that takes me everywhere.

Question: Good that's one.

Barbara: And I do have food in my refrigerator.

Question: Good that's another one.

Barbara: And I do have money in the bank.

Question: Good that's another one.

Barbara: And I have friends who help me... and children...

Question: Well it seems like you can find many ways that life is supporting you...

Barbara: Yes.

Question: So how does that feel?

Barbara: Nice...

Question: So the next time the thought arises that *life doesn't support me...* you might not feel so freaked out by it. And after a while, when the thought arises, you might just laugh.

Barbara: Yes, I can see that... it's such a nice feeling right now.

Question: I see another turnaround...

Barbara: Yes I do too ... *I don't support me...* or rather... *My thinking doesn't support me!*

Question: Could that be as true or truer?

Barbara: Yes obviously! It's my thinking that's driving me crazy!

Question: Nice to know also—that it's not life but your thinking that is not supporting you!

So you can now see that by doing the Work on the belief that *life doesn't support me*, I came to realize that life really is supporting me—in so many ways! And now, when I go back to the focus tool on page 103 and do the exercise we call "Notice the support"—I really do believe it because I know that it's the truth! Now noticing the support is such a powerful meditation for me. I just love it because I really believe it now!

So this is why I say, if you are using focus tools, it is a good idea to investigate the beliefs you may have that are contradicting the focus tools and which are preventing you from experiencing the full power of the goodness of life!

Looking at the body

Now here's another session with me... for your entertainment and enlightenment. This time it's about the body. And when you read through the session, please look within and find your own thoughts about your body and answer the questions for yourself.

So here we go. Here's a thought about my body that's bothering me and which might be bothering you too. The thought is: *My body shouldn't have aches and pains.*

So let's do "The Work" on this thought *my body shouldn't have aches and pains.*

Question: So Barbara, is it true that your body shouldn't have aches and pains? (Question 1).

Barbara: Yes, it's true. I don't want my body to have aches and pains. My life would be better if my body didn't have aches and pains. (This is a good sub-thought to investigate next.)

Question: OK Barbara, so can you absolutely know that it's true that your body shouldn't have aches and pains? (Question 2). Because what's the reality? Does your body have aches and pains?

Barbara: Yes my body does have ache and pains, so the answer to the question is—no, I can't absolutely know that it's true because the reality is my body does have aches and pains.

Question: So how does it make you feel when you believe the thought that your body shouldn't have aches and pains Barbara and it does? (Question 3—how do you feel when you believe this thought?)

Barbara: Well I feel terrible and I worry that maybe something serious is wrong with me and that I won't be able to function and make money. I feel my whole survival is threatened by the fact that my body has aches and pains. (Good sub-thoughts to investigate.)

Question: That must be very stressful.

Barbara: Yes it is. It really scares me a lot and then I really do notice every little ache and pain!

Question: So who would you be if you could not believe the thought that *your body shouldn't have aches and pains when it does?*

Barbara: Well I'd be a lot more relaxed because I would accept the fact that my body is aching and then I'd guess I'd try to find out why and deal with it as best I can.

Question: Wouldn't that be a less stressful way to live?

Barbara: Yes it really would.

Question: So turn the thought around.

Barbara: *My body should have aches and pains.*

Question: So could that be as true as or truer than your original statement?

Barbara: Yes obviously because my body does have aches and pains.

Question: So that's the reality.

Barbara: Yes.

Question: So Barbara, give me three specific examples of why your body should have aches and pains.

Barbara: Well maybe my body is telling me to take better care of myself.

Question: That sounds logical. So maybe you should listen!

Barbara: Yes I guess I should.

Question: OK another example of why your body should have aches and pains.

Barbara: Well it forces me to take better care of myself.

Question: Really? So you mean without your body aching you wouldn't be taking such good care of yourself? Isn't that interesting to notice!

Barbara: Yes it really is. I never thought about that before.

Question: Well nice body.

Barbara: Yes.

Question: OK another reason why your body should have aches and pains?

Barbara: Well it forces me to slow down and that's good for me too.

Question: Really. You mean without your body aching you wouldn't slow down?

Barbara: Probably not.

Question: Interesting.

Barbara: Yeah and when I slow down I actually do get to enjoy the present moment.

Question: Very interesting. So you are saying that without this body of yours aching, you would miss the present moment?

Barbara: Probably.

Question: Sounds to me like you should thank your lucky stars that your body is aching! Are you saying without these aches and pains you wouldn't notice the present moment?

Barbara: Probably! I know it's embarrassing but it's true!

Question: Anything else?

Barbara: Well since my body is aching, I went to bed with a good spiritual book that I probably wouldn't have had time to read if my body was OK and I really got some fantastic insights into the Nature of Reality. And this new understanding makes me so happy!

Question: My goodness! So Barbara, can you hear what you are saying?

Barbara: Well yes, sort of.

Question: So let me ask you this… if the only way the goodness of life could come to you is through your aching body… do you still want your body not to ache!

Barbara: Wow!

Resisting reality hurts

So as you can see, investigating your thinking, investigating the thoughts that are really bothering you, slowly and carefully, can really lead you to the most amazing insights! And you may actually discover, if you take your time, why in fact your life is better because things are like they are.

But whatever you do, when you investigate your thinking, you will discover just how much it hurts to resist reality. You discover that it really makes you suffer because you can't change reality. Reality is what it is. Life is what it is. And you begin to see how when you think reality should be different than what it is, you are setting yourself up to feel bad. You can see that this is a natural law. When your thinking is out of harmony with reality, you suffer. When your thinking is in harmony with the way things are, you feel peaceful and good. It's as simple as that. There's no mystery to it. It's mechanical law you could say.

But most of us don't know this yet. So what do we do? Most of the time, we just argue with reality and feel bad. And since we just don't see what we're doing, we think life is doing it to us. But it's not. We're doing it to ourselves. We're the ones who are making ourselves feel bad. And this is what most of us do most of the time. And it goes like this. We think people should be different than they are—and then we wonder why we have such a hard time getting along with them. We think life should be different than it is—and then we wonder why we feel that life is such a struggle. We think our bodies should look and feel different than they are—and then we are unkind to ourselves and beat ourselves up instead of taking good care of ourselves and nurturing ourselves. We think our parents and children should be different than they are—and then we wonder why it hurts so much to be in their company. And we think our partners should be different too... and everyone knows what that gets you!

The battle with reality hurts!

Resisting reality hurts!

It really does.

And who does it hurt?

You! Me!

Us!

So this is why I say if you want to live a happy life, it's a good idea to investigate all the stories and beliefs you have that argue with reality. Write down your beliefs and question them and find out if they are true. Find out if there's any reality to them at all! Find out where you are resisting life. Find out where your thoughts are out of harmony with what is. And just notice what you find. And then see what happens to your life!

Reality check: It's a law

When your thinking is out of harmony with reality, you suffer. When your thinking is in harmony with the way things are, you feel peaceful and good. It's as simple as that.

Investigation tool no. 3: Focusing on the real

Here is a meditation/focusing technique that helps break catastrophic thinking and bring you back to reality. When catastrophic thinking takes over, we scare ourselves by projecting into the future and imagining scary scenarios that probably will never happen. We get upset and panic because our minds are bombarding us with a stream of "what ifs?" and we believe them! We feel overwhelmed by our own fearful projections of what might happen in the future and suddenly life may feel unmanageable. When this happens, the body reacts to our thinking with a host of symptoms. The heart pounds, we sweat, we feel shaky, dizzy, and so forth. The body's normal "fight or flight" reaction sets in.

A really good and extremely simple technique to break spiraling catastrophic thinking and the unpleasant physical sensations that go with it is to make up your mind to focus on the real in the simplest and most practical sense of the word. And by this I mean, wherever you are and whatever you are doing, look at what is right before you, right there where you are. Turn your attention away from your catastrophic thinking and start naming the objects, things, items, people whatever it is that is there within your field of awareness. (Later, when you calm down and are safe at home, you can write down the thoughts that are scaring you and investigate them using the four questions described above). But now, in the crisis situation, a good technique is to focus on this moment.

Let's take an example. Say for example, you are sitting in the waiting room at the dentist's office and you're pretty scared because you know you are going to have a tooth filled. You are afraid of going to the dentist. So your heart is starting to pound because you are afraid of the thought of being stuck in the dentist chair, you are afraid that it will hurt. You know that the dentist will give you a shot of novocaine so it doesn't hurt. But that thought doesn't help much because you're afraid of needles and just the thought of the dentist coming over to you with that big needle makes you feel like fainting. What if you faint in the dentist's chair? You feel yourself starting to sweat and your heart is pounding rapidly. The more you think about it, the worse you feel. And absolutely nothing has happened so far. The reality is you are sitting quietly in the waiting room. That's reality. But in your mind, you're on your way straight to hell!

When something like this happens and you start to panic, it's difficult (if not impossible) to tell yourself to stop worrying and thinking about these things. That almost never works because obviously you wouldn't be thinking about it if you could stop! Nobody likes to torture themselves on purpose. And as I said before, it will probably be too difficult for you to sit there calmly and question your catastrophic thinking (but please remember to do it when you are relaxed at home!). But right now, you can use the power of your mind wisely and make the conscious decision to switch your attention to what is really going on right where you are. This you probably can do because it is so simple.

So here's what to do. Just start by naming (slowly) all the things you see right where you are. Now back to our example of the waiting room. Just start naming whatever is in the waiting room. Start, for example, with the nice little table next to your chair. Look at it. Say to yourself, here's a nice little table. On the table there are three magazines. One Vogue and one Cosmopolitan and one travel guide. You can even pick each one up and put it down again. Continue your investigation of the room—of the now. Next to the table is a big fish tank. In the fish tank, there are seven gold fish—two big fat ones and five smaller ones. One of the fish has a big tail. There are three other dark fishes too plus some green plants swaying nicely in the tank too. The fish are swimming around peacefully. The water is bubbling in the corner of the tank. There are some rocks in the tank too, on the bottom. And next to the tank, on the other side of the tank, there is a man sitting on a chair reading a magazine. He is wearing jeans and Adidas running shoes. His hair is black. He's got a backpack with him and it's on the floor next to his chair. He looks like he's about 40. Next to him there is a magazine stand with lots more magazines like National Geographic... and so on you go. Slowly and quietly, you continue naming the reality that is right in from of your eyes. Focusing your attention quietly on each object and person, naming each as your attention rests on it. You are focusing on what is real, what is here, what is now. You are not off somewhere in your imagination. You are here, now, in this room. It is very calming to do this. And if you find your mind wandering back to your catastrophic thinking while you are doing this, just bring your focus back again on the next thing in the room.

If you want to make this exercise even more effective, you can add a calming breathing technique to it. As you are slowly looking around and naming objects and people, breathe in deeply counting to four slowly (four seconds) and breathe out slowly counting to four seconds. This slow breathing, if done for at least four minutes or about 24 breaths, works wonders when it comes to calming the body and slowing down your rapidly beating heart! It has a medically proven calming effect because when we are nervous we often hyperventilate which changes the chemical balance of the blood (making us feel weird, shaky, etc.) and this slow breathing helps normalize the chemical balance again.

**Investigation tool no. 4: Focusing on this step /
My train trip to Malmø technique**

Here's another good variation of the above present-moment awareness technique I've developed. You can use this variation when you are on your way to a situation you fear or are worried about. Again it's all about sticking to the present moment, to reality and not getting lost in your fearful thoughts. (And again, please investigate the thoughts that frighten you as soon as you can.)

I call this technique "my train trip to Malmø technique" and it's all about being mindful of this moment. Here's an example of how it works: You live in Copenhagen and you have to go to an important meeting in Malmø (the Swedish town on the other side of the Sound). You're nervous because you have to make a presentation when you get there. It will take you about an hour and 30 minutes to get to the meeting. First you have to go to the station and take the train to Malmø and then when you arrive in Malmø you have to take a taxi to the company where the presentation is going to be held. So all in all, it will be about an hour and a half from your office to the place where you're giving the presentation. You really don't feel like going but you can't back out now. But you're so nervous about making the presentation that you've been seriously thinking about calling and cancelling all day.

Here's where the "focusing on this step" technique can help. Start by saying to yourself, "OK I'm a free human being and I can cancel at any time. No one can force me to go to Malmø and give this presentation. I can do whatever I want. And right now I'm just going to put on my coat and walk over to the train station and see how that feels. Right now I'm just going to forget everything else and focus on walking over there. When I get to the station, if I really feel terrible, I can always call and cancel. But right now I'm just going to walk to the station. That's all I have to do." Then walk over to the station and just focus on that. Drop all other thoughts. Just notice everything you can about walking to the station. The sidewalk, the weather, how the cold air feels, how the ground feels under your feet as you walk to the station. Stay in this moment. Notice the people passing by. Then when you get to the station, see how you feel. You'll probably see that you feel pretty much the same when you get there. No better, no worse. So when you get there, you can say to yourself. "OK I know I am a free human being and I can cancel at any time. Right now I'm just going to buy my ticket and go down to the railway platform and see how that feels. When I get down to the platform, if I feel really terrible, I can always turn around and go home." Then buy your ticket and go down to the platform, focusing only on that. Notice the ticket seller and the counter in as many details as you can. Stay in the present moment. Watch yourself paying for the ticket and going down the escalator to the platform. Then when you are down on the platform, see how you feel. You'll probably see that you feel pretty much the same when you get down there. No better, no worse. Nothing has really happened. You were just walking. So now you can say to yourself. "OK, I'll see what happens when the train comes. If I feel really terrible when the train pulls in, I will just turn around and go home." Then focus on this moment, the platform, the other people waiting, the cold air. Notice the billboards and the lights. When the train comes in, you'll probably see that you feel pretty much the same. No better, no worse. Nothing's going on at all. You're just standing there waiting. If any thoughts of your meeting and presentation come into your mind, just go back to looking at the platform and the people waiting for the train. Stay in this moment. Now when the train approaches you can say to yourself, "OK, well I'll get on the train and sit down. I can always get off at the next stop if I feel any worse, but right now I'm just going to focus on getting on and finding a seat." Then do that. Focus on that task, on the task at hand. Watch yourself getting onto the train and sitting down. Notice how nice the seat is and how cozy it feels to be in the warm train after standing on the cold platform. Again stay in the moment and notice that nothing is really going on. A few minutes ago you were standing on the platform, now you're sitting in a seat. That's about it. You're still breathing. Life is still going on. Notice the inside of the train and the other people. Keep yourself in the present moment. If any thoughts of your meeting and presentation come to mind, just return your attention to the people sitting across from you. Study everything in detail. Notice, really notice, what's happening in this moment. You'll probably find yourself relaxing so much that you can lose yourself in the magazine you brought along for a while. If any thoughts of the meeting and presentation come into your mind, you can say to yourself, "OK well when I get to Malmø, if I feel any worse, I can always take the train right back home. But right now, I'm just going to read my magazine."

When the train arrives in Malmø after 45 minutes, you can say to yourself, "OK, I'm going to get off the train and walk into the station and see how that feels. I'm just going to focus on that and if I feel terrible when I get inside the station, I can just turn around and take the train back to Copenhagen. That's about as bad as it can get." Then do that and stay with that. Watch yourself getting up from your seat and walking to the door. Then get off the train and walk with the rest of the people into the station. Notice the rush of cold air as you step off the train. Stay with this moment. Then when you enter the station...

And just keep yourself in the present moment, the whole way through. Every step of the way, detail by detail, situation by situation, moment by moment. And that's about it. I know it sounds very simple, but when you try it, you will see how difficult it can be. Because we spend so much time in our minds, projecting into a future that's just not happening anywhere except in our heads!

So this whole exercise is about staying present in this moment instead of driving yourself crazy with stories about something that's coming up in the future. And the thing about consciously using this technique is that you discover that this is actually a very sensible way to live your life—whether or not you're worried and anxious about something!

To actually be aware and mindful of what's actually going on right now is really what the art of living is all about. It's called being present in your life! It's called waking up to reality, which can only be now!

Trying an exercise like this (for example when you're nervous) will make you realize how seldom you are really awake to this present moment and what's going on around you right now.

So give it a try and see what you discover.

And don't forget to question your catastrophic thinking when you get home and feel calm again. What is it that is so stressful about this situation? What is it you fear? Why are you so upset? What is your story? Write it all down and investigate the thoughts that scare you. Is there a difference between reality and your thoughts?

Relationships

Relationships are another area of our lives where there is very often a big difference between our stories and expectations and reality. And this causes us endless heartache and suffering. What happens to so many of us is that we have a long list of ideas about what our partners "should" or "shouldn't" do or what we "should" or "shouldn't" do to make our relationships work. And then we try to live this—and it never works! Because once again, when we fight reality, when we resist the way things are—and in this case, the way our partners really are—we set ourselves up for unhappiness and failure. Because reality is what it is, people are who they are. (And once again, I'm not saying you can't ask for what you want!) But the reality is your partner is who he or she is. Did you take a close look before you signed up for partnership or did you think that with a little work, you could make this person into the partner of your dreams?

To help clarify some of these issues, I've developed a relationship exercise that I call "Expectations versus reality" which we have been using at our lectures and workshops. In this exercise, you can explore the difference between your expectations to your partner and reality. Participants get really excited about the discoveries they make and often come up to us afterwards to thank us for the amazing insights they found. So you might want to give it a try. Here it is!

Investigation tool no. 5: Expectations versus reality

This exercise has four parts. You can do this exercise on your own or with another person. (I suggest you do not do this with your partner because it is important to be able to be completely honest. It's OK if you do it with a friend, as long as it's someone you can really be honest with.)

If you are not in a relationship at the moment, you can still do this exercise and learn a lot. Do it on your ex-partner. And if you've never had a relationship, use your mother! (It works just as well!)

Now please get out a piece of paper.

Part One: Expectations and wishes

Close your eyes and think of at least three things you wish your present partner would do (or that your ex-partner should have done). Think of three important things you think he or she "should" do now or should have done in the past that would make (or have made) your relationship better.

Here are some examples of what I mean. You might feel:

- He should spend more time with the children. (Or he should have.)
- He should stop drinking (he shouldn't drink so much).
- He should understand me better.

- He should be interested in the things I'm interested in.

Once you have thought of three important things that you really believe would make your relationship better, write the three things down on a piece of paper. (If you are doing this alone, you can of course write down more than three things). If you are doing this exercise with another person, take turns telling each other about the three things you wrote on your list. When you are listening to the other person tell about his or her three things, don't come with your opinion as to whether he/she is right or wrong. Just listen and allow the other person to tell you his or her story.

Part Two: Reality

The next step in the exercise is to close your eyes and think of what the reality is compared to the three things you wrote on your list. Really go there. Look at what the actual situation is in relation to your expectations and wishes. Once you have identified what the reality is about each of your expectations, write it down on your paper.

In terms of the examples I gave above in Part One, the reality could look like this:

- He doesn't spend a lot of time with the children. (Or he does play with the children sometimes, but not as much as I would like).
- He drinks a lot. (Or he drinks too much. Or he has a serious alcohol problem.)
- He doesn't understand me. (Or sometimes he understands me.)
- He's not interested in the things I'm interested in. (Or sometimes he is interested and sometimes not. It depends on what it is.)

Now if you are doing this exercise with another person, take turns telling each other about the reality compared to your expectations. Tell in detail what you discovered when you looked at the way things really are. And again, when you are listening to the other person tell about his or her reality, just listen and allow the other person to tell you what he or she discovered. There is no right and wrong here. This is just an exploration of the way things are.

Part Three: Feelings

In part three, close your eyes and imagine how you would feel about your relationship and your partner if you were realistic. How would you feel if you accepted what the reality is? How would you feel if you didn't have any expectations or wishes that anything should be different from what it is? How would this feel? Go into the feelings. I have discovered that this step of the exercise can take a little time. It can take a little time to locate how you would feel if you related to the way things really are. I've discovered this is true because so many of our feelings about our relationships are linked to our expectations! We feel upset or sad or angry because of our expectations, so in this step, when you take them away, what do you actually feel? Try to find that...

Then once you've found how that makes you feel, please write down these feelings. It can often be an eye-opener to discover one would feel quite differently!

And if you are working with a partner, now tell each other about the feelings you discovered when you thought about how you would feel if you accepted reality when it comes to the way your partner is. And once again, no judgments, just listen to each other.

Part Four: Action

The last step of the exercise is to look at what these discoveries lead to. So close your eyes again. Now that you've really felt what it would feel like if you accepted things the way they really are, how are you going to act? What actions do these feelings make you want to take? If you stick to reality, what will you do? What will you do differently right now if you look reality in the eye and forget your wishes and expectations?

And if you are doing this exercise on an ex-partner, when you go back into the past, try to find how you would have acted differently in your former relationship if you really had looked at reality and acted accordingly. What would you have done differently?

Now write down what you would do—and especially what you will do differently than what you're doing now (or what you did in the past). This is called waking up to reality! This is "getting real". This is looking at what is and dealing with it—instead of living in some dream world. Sit with your discoveries for a while. How does this feel?

And if you are working with a partner; talk to your partner about the actions that come to mind that you feel are realistic in terms of reality. What is the realistic thing for you to do now?

I have noticed that people make wildly different discoveries when doing this exercise. Some people discover a new sense of appreciation for their partners—a new kindness—when they look at who their partners really are (instead of their stories about their partners). And they say they are going to be much more appreciative and loving in the future. Others say that now they're definitely going to leave their partner because it's so obvious that things are never going to change!

Whatever you do find, welcome to reality! It was there all along. It was just us who didn't notice.

* * *

For more about understanding the difference between reality and our thoughts, stories and expectations in our relationships, see Tim's book *"101 Myths about Relationships that Drive Us Crazy – and a Little about What You Can Do about Them"*. Check out our Web site for more details: www.beamteam.com.

* * *

You are not your thoughts or stories

In conclusion, it is important to remember that *you are not your thoughts or your stories!* Even though you may be so strongly identified with and attached to your stories that you haven't noticed this, the truth is you are not your stories. You *have* stories, but they are not what you are. Remember Law 2—the Law of Witnessing (page 26). This law tells us that you are able to watch thoughts arising and disappearing while you remain. And this means that since you are able to witness your thoughts as they come and go, you are not your thoughts. This is a key concept to remember because it means you don't have to identify with your stories! It means you can stand back and pinpoint your stories and then, if they are making you unhappy, you can question them. You can take a close look at them and see if they are true. You can ask yourself if your stories have anything to do with the way things are. You can ask yourself if your stories correspond in any way with reality—or are they just dreams, illusions? This understanding, the understanding that you are not your thoughts but the universal consciousness in which all thoughts arise, gives you freedom from the tyranny of your own thinking. This understanding gives you the ability to use the power of your mind wisely and question your thinking. And this is a major shift, a dramatic shift because it means you are no longer being run by your stories. Instead you are learning to question and free yourself from the tyranny of your own thinking! What a wonderful relief!

PART THREE: IN YOUR LIFE

PUTTING IT ALL INTO PRACTICE

Putting it all to work in your life

In this section, we're going to look at the various ways you can put all this information to work in your life.

The daily program

As I've said many times before, it's not enough to just read this book (or any other good book) or go to lectures and workshops. You must put these ideas and concepts into practice in your daily life. It's not enough to read about meditation, you have to meditate. It's not enough to talk about focus tools, you have to use them. It's not enough to understand the importance of mindfulness; you have to practice being mindful. It's not enough to know you should investigate your stories; you have to actually do it!

So to help you on your way, we have developed some scenarios for a daily program so you can find a level of daily practice which suits your needs and lifestyle. Remember, if you practice a little, you can expect some small results. If you practice moderately, you can expect moderate results. If you practice whole heartedly with dedication, you can expect even better results.

Elements of the daily program

Your daily program can be made up of various elements, depending on your situation, needs and preferences. Here are some of the different elements a daily program can include:

- Gratitude (Power questions, making gratitude lists, noticing the support)
- Meditation or a mindfulness practice

- Contemplation (for example contemplating the Nature of Reality) or mental treatment (scientific prayer)
- The four questions of the Work
- Reading and studying (See suggested reading on page 201)
- Going in nature
- Silence
- Dancing and singing to uplifting music
- Service (helping others—not for pay) (see page 175)

Suggested daily programs

Below are some suggested daily programs we present at our workshops. The programs are divided into three levels—Light, Regular and Turbo.

Getting Real Light (Once a day x 20 minutes)

Here are three examples of a possible "light" daily program. Pick the one that suits you best or design another one using one or more of the tools listed above.

Program A: 10 minutes meditation + 10 minutes contemplation or mental treatment

Program B: 10 minutes silence + 10 minutes gratitude (Power questions or making a gratitude list)

Program C: Read and study for 10 minutes + 10 minutes meditation

In addition to one of the above programs, add:

Once a week for at least 20 minutes: Work with the four questions of the Work

Once a week for at least 20 minutes: Walk in nature in silence (no talking)

Getting Real Regular (Twice a day x 20 minutes)

Here are three examples of a possible "regular" daily program. Pick the one that suits you best or design another one using one or more of the tools listed above.

Program A: 20 minutes meditation, 10 minutes contemplation or mental treatment + 10 minutes gratitude (Power questions or making a gratitude list)

Program B: 20 minutes meditation, 20 minutes working with the four questions of the Work

Program C: 20 minutes reading and studying, 20 minutes meditation

In addition to one of the above programs, add:

Once a week for at least 1 hour: Walking in nature in silence (no talking)

Once a week for at least 1 hour: Work with the four questions of the Work

Once a week for at least 1 hour: Service (helping others—not for pay)

Getting Real Turbo (Three or four times a day x 30 minutes)

Here are two examples of a possible "turbo" daily program. Pick the one that suits you best or design another one using one or more of the tools listed above.

Program A: 20 minutes meditation + 10 minutes contemplation or mental treatment, 30 minutes reading and studying, 30 minutes the four questions of the Work

In addition, add:

Once a week for at least 1 hour: Walking in nature in silence (no talking).

Once a week for at least 1 hour: Working with the four questions of the Work

Once a week for at least 1 hour: Service (helping others—not for pay)

Program B: 30 minutes contemplation, 30 minutes meditation, 30 minutes working with the four questions of the Work, 30 minutes reading and studying

In addition, add:

Once a week for at least 3 hours: Walking in nature in silence (no talking)
Once a week for at least 3 hours: Working with the four questions of the Work
Once a week for at least 1-3 hours: Service (helping others—not for pay)

You can also mix the daily programs during the course of a week. For example, you can do the "regular" program on weekends when you have more time and the "light" version during the week when you are very busy. And then of course you can try the "turbo" version when you are on holiday!

Important points to remember
When working with a daily program it is important to remember the following points:

- Do it regularly (every day).
- It's better to do a little every day than to do a lot once in a while.
- Moderation.
- It's better to do a little each day and be successful than to try to do a lot and give up because it's too much.
- It's important to design a program that fits your lifestyle and your daily life.
- Be flexible. You can mix the daily programs during the course of your week.

The process
When we start this process and begin to wake up to reality and become more conscious about the way the mind works, we are unleashing a radical and dramatic shift in our consciousness and lifestyle which will continue for the rest of our lives. When this happens, you can never go back to your old way of thinking,

living and coping with life again. It's like trying to put toothpaste back into the tube—it's impossible! You have now set yourself on a course towards increased freedom and joy—and there's simply no turning back.

So congratulations!

But this is not to say the journey will not be challenging. The reality is—the journey is challenging—and sometimes very challenging! Of course it's different for everyone because everyone is different. Some people go through rapid and dramatic change, often because they're in crisis already, while others move through the process much more slowly. And other people seem to advance in leaps and then remain at a certain plateau for years. So remember everyone is different and don't judge what's happening to you by comparing your process to other people's processes. Your process is yours. Your journey is yours—and uniquely so.

So what happens?

When you begin a dedicated process of waking up to reality you usually feel better and worse at the same time! You feel better because you are gaining new insight and using the various techniques which make a real difference in your life. You feel a new sense of peace and clarity—and new energy. It's wonderful!

And then you also feel worse! And this feeling worse usually comes in waves.

So why do you also feel worse?

You feel worse because as you wake up, you become aware of all the negative and stressful thoughts, beliefs and stories you have been run by your whole life. It's like all your old programming and your old belief system starts to come to the surface—with all the emotions that are linked to this. And at times this can be very painful and emotional.

So what can we do about this?

One of the first things we discover is that our old coping

strategies are no longer the best solution. Previously because we didn't understand how the mind works, we had a tendency to go into denial and try to suppress the thoughts and emotions we were afraid of. We did this because we didn't have the understanding or the appropriate tools to deal with them, so we usually tried to suppress painful thoughts and emotions by running away from them. And if that didn't work, we tried to distract ourselves through our favorite addictions—like television, alcohol, drugs, sex, shopping, eating, or work... you name it. Most of us have been experts at distracting ourselves from our deepest fears by drowning ourselves in working or sex or food or alcohol...

But now with our new insights, we are better able to understand what is happening to us and we can also see that our old coping strategies probably won't help. In fact, in most cases they will only make things worse!

So what can we do?

The enlightened way to deal with this process is first of all to realize that *this is a process*. Just to realize this can help so much. Just to realize that what you are experiencing is a natural part of the process of waking up to reality can be such a comfort. And then remind yourself that most people don't just wake up one day and are completely free and clear! It doesn't happen like that. Most of us really have to work hard at it and for many of us it can at times be very frightening. Also because there are not many people in our society who understand what the process of waking up to reality entails.

So *understanding and acceptance* are the number one priority. Accept that this is what is happening to you. Accept that it's not always going to be easy. Accept that sometimes you are going to feel great and that sometimes you are going to feel really lousy. That's just how it works! And realize that when you feel lousy, it doesn't mean there's something wrong with you or that you're doing something wrong. It probably just means that the old programming is coming to the surface to be released. And this means *the more you resist it, the more it persists!* And this is a very important point to remember—*what you resist persists.* The more you struggle against the changes that are going on inside you, the more you struggle against the painful thoughts and emotions that are coming to the surface, the stronger they become. In fact, your resistance adds energy to them. So the best thing you can do is to let these thoughts and emotions just arise and see them for what they are—old patterns and old programming coming to the surface to be released.

> What you resist, persists.

If possible, be like water and just allow the process to flow through you. This is the safest and easiest thing to do. Without your resistance, without attaching to the unpleasant thoughts and emotions, these thoughts and emotions will just come for a while and then go again. In situations like this, you can shift your attention to the witness, the observer, your true self and just allow what ever is happening to happen.

It's also a good idea to remind yourself that whatever is happening is what should be happening because it is happening! And remember that everything is working for you, everything is unfolding for you! And then use your tools! Use the techniques described in this book. Stick to your daily program. Exercise discipline. Use the four questions of the Work, especially when you feel overwhelmed by negative thoughts and emotions. Write the thoughts down on paper and question them. Find out if there's any truth to the things that are bothering you. Do the Work for breakfast, lunch and dinner until you start to feel a little clearer again.

Keep on reading and studying.

And keep doing the other practices described in this book. Yes I know it requires discipline, especially when you're feeling bad. And of course if you are unable to deal with your problems on your own, please seek professional help! Seeking help is not a sign of failure. Seeking help may be the very best and wisest way you can take care of yourself if your life situation seems overwhelming. Remember this process of waking up to reality and "getting real" as we call it, is also about learning to take care of yourself. Taking care of you is your job! It's your responsibility. This is also one the great "learnings" in all this. It's all about you. And it's all up to you. So ask for help if you need it—either from friends or from a professional.

Whatever happens, you will soon discover that the periods when you feel bad come and go. They never come to stay! They just come for a while and you get to experience them—and then they go again. Always!

A support team

In terms of help and support, it is so important to have people around you who understand what you are doing and what you're going through. The ideal situation is to have a support team or to be in a community or with a group of like-minded people who are also going through this process. In this way, you can help and support each other when the going gets tough.

If your life situation is not like this, see if you can't find at least one other person you can connect with about these matters. Perhaps by going to lectures or workshops or joining a meditation group, you will meet someone who you can share your process with. Because it's a great help if you have someone you can call and talk to when your old stuff starts coming to the surface.

We believe that it is so important to have support during this process that we always encourage participants at our workshops to make contact with each other and sign up to be each other's "getting real buddies" after the workshop experience. We encourage them to call and support each other in their processes. We've heard from people that this is a great help so please try to find someone you can connect with. Again because the reality is we live in a society, which has very little awareness when it comes to these matters and this can make the whole process more difficult, especially if you feel very alone and isolated. So be good to yourself and make an effort to find someone you can talk to about your process. It's usually a great help.

Service

Another good way to help yourself is service or helping others! And by service and helping others, we mean "not-for-pay" activities, in other words, any activity where you give your time and energy to help other people for free.

As we wake up to reality, we come to see that all of Life is One, interconnected web and that we are all one family, so it is only natural to want to contribute and do something loving, kind, and helpful for others. We realize that by helping others, we are helping ourselves since we are all One! You could call this "enlightened selfishness"! But in reality, this is love in action. This is the love in our hearts expressing itself. This is our true nature, this is who we are. And when we do something for others—not for our own immediate, personal gain but from the love in our hearts—we always feel better, no matter how rotten we might have felt to begin with! Also dedicating some time to service is a good way to get the right perspective on your own problems and challenges. If you need to distract yourself and take a break from you—service is a great way to do it!

This is why service is part of our suggested daily programs above. Doing something for others on a regular basis is definitely an enlightened way to feel better. So give it a try. Make up your mind to do something definite and concrete at least once a week to help someone else. And during the course of your day when the opportunity arises to assist another person, do so! Let the goodness of your heart flow! It's the best medicine.

Reality check: How can I serve?

It's really quite easy to find out how you can help in almost every situation. Just shift your focus from "what's in it for me?" to "how can I serve, help or contribute in this situation?" and see what happens.

Changing the world

As you read this book, you might at times have been asking yourself questions like this: "What about the rest of the world? What about other people? This whole project about me waking up to reality, is it really just about me? Isn't this a selfish way to live? What about the world situation? Wouldn't it be better if I dedicated my life to helping others instead of worrying about myself?"

It's a very interesting question isn't it, because of course when we are really in touch with the love in our hearts, our natural impulse is to want to do something to alleviate the suffering we see around us. But the big question of course is how? How can we help relieve and alleviate the suffering we see everywhere? What is the best way, the most effective way?

If you look carefully, you will discover that many people are dedicating their lives and all their energy to working for change in the world around them—be it through social service, politics, government or business. And of course, this is a high-minded and wonderful endeavor which I definitely salute.

Out there is a reflection of *in here*
But there is another view or way of looking at it when it comes to

our desire to alleviate the suffering we see around us. And we discover that view when we begin this process of waking up to reality. Because one of the things we find is that the world around us is the result of the sum total of all the thoughts, beliefs and stories of all the human beings who have walked this earth. *Out there* is the perfect and exact reflection of what we have *in here*. The suffering we see *out there* is the mirror image of the suffering we have *in here*. The greed we see *out there* is the mirror image of the greed we have *in here*. And the same goes for all the fear, intolerance, confusion, ignorance, anxiety and anger we see around us. It is all the mirror image of what we have *in here*. And by *in here,* I mean the thoughts and beliefs we all are entertaining whether we are conscious of it or not. Whether we are aware of it or not, the world around us is the result of all our beliefs and programming. How could it be otherwise?

When we understand this we can also see that the world will never change until we change. That is why, if we really and truly want to work for a better world—a world that is the embodiment of the peace and love we all desire—the best place to start is with making peace within yourself! How could it be otherwise? How can you expect the world to be a world of peace and beauty and tolerance and grace and love, if you yourself are a seething cauldron of fear, anger, confusion, and anxiety? How could it happen? Where should the love come from if not from you? When you understand this, you see that you're the one! You're the one who has to change the world. Yes, you're the one! So work on yourself—and amazingly enough you will discover that as you change, your world will change too.

The suffering we see *out there*
is the mirror image
of the suffering we have *in here*.

You and the world: The ripple effect

I call this the ripple effect. When you work on yourself, when you do inner work, your world will begin to reflect back to you the changes going on inside yourself. It works like this:

You are a conscious human being who has thoughts and beliefs. Your underlying beliefs and thoughts about this thing we call life determine your world view. Your world view determines your morality and ethics or you could say your world view *is* your morality and ethics. Your morals and ethics determine the way you talk and act. The way you talk and act influences and determines all your relationships—your relationships with your family and friends, your relationships at work, your relationships in your community. All these relationships are determined by your thoughts and beliefs which result in the way your talk and act. Thus you can see that your underlying beliefs are the direct cause of your influence on your relationships and the world around you—your environment and the world.

In this way you can see that by doing inner work and becoming clear, by working with your own thoughts and beliefs, you are changing the way you interact with and influence the world around you. As you change, as you wake up to reality and become a kinder, more peaceful and loving person, your interactions with all the people you meet changes. And this in turn influences them and their thoughts and ways of interacting with other people, which in turn influences your community and yes your world.

Reality check: The ripple effect

You → your underlying beliefs and thoughts → your morality and ethics (your world view) → your speech and actions → your close relationships → your interactions at work → your interactions in your community → society → the world

BONUS TRACKS

BOLLUM TALKS TO BARBARA

When you read the transcripts of conversations I sometimes have in my head (on the following pages) between the part of me that is waking up to reality and the part of me that is still confused, you will see that I'm just like Smeagol/Gollum in "The Lord of the Rings". Does this sound familiar?

Bollum talks to Barbara – about being productive

Bollum: You really should get up off your sofa Barbara and get to work. You've got books to write and things to do.

Barbara: But lying here is so blissful.

Bollum: Blissful? Who needs blissful, you've got to work! Be productive, make money, achieve! You can't do that lying on your sofa!

Barbara: But lying here is so blissful! Isn't that what the Spiritual Pathway is about anyway? Being present in the moment?

Bollum: Well you can do that when you get old.

Barbara: But I am old!

Bollum: Well not old enough.

Barbara: Well if I keep on waiting, I'll be dead by the time I have time to enjoy the bliss of being here now.

Bollum: Oh come on girl. Pull yourself together. You don't deserve to live unless you are productive.

Barbara: Really? You're making me nervous.

Bollum: You should be with your work ethic! If everyone was like you the whole world would go under.

Barbara: Is that true?

Bollum: Sure it's true. How will you ever get a big house on the beach?

Barbara: What do I need a big house on the beach for?

Bollum: Well it's a sign of success and happiness.

Barbara: Is that true? What does a big house have to do with happiness? I'm feeling perfectly happy right now lying on my sofa.

Bollum: You're hopeless. You'll never be a success.

Bollum talks to Barbara – about staring at a blank wall

Bollum: What are you doing Barbara?

Barbara: I'm sitting, looking at a blank wall.

Bollum: WHAT?

Barbara: And breathing...

Bollum: You're doing what?

Barbara: I'm meditating.

Bollum: Meditating? Sounds like you're wasting time to me. You should be doing something productive.

Barbara: I am.

Bollum: You call sitting and staring at a white wall doing something productive?

Barbara: Yes.

Bollum: What is productive about what you are doing?

Barbara: I'm watching my mind.

Bollum: Watching your mind? What good is that?

Barbara: Well it's helping me understand the nature of mind and this thing called life.

Bollum: You don't need to understand anything Barbara, all you need to do is get busy. That's the only way to achieve anything in this life.

Barbara: Are you sure about that?

Bollum: Of course I'm sure. How do you think famous people get famous?

Barbara: Why would I want to be famous?

Bollum: Everyone wants to be famous.

Barbara: Really? What good will fame do me or anyone else?

Bollum: Well then you can get on TV and people will listen to what you have to say.

Barbara: And what will I have to say if I'm so busy running around that I'm never present in this moment?

Bollum: OK, OK, but right now, I think you've had enough of this staring at the white wall business for today. You can't do this every day... I mean what will people think?

Barbara: So now you want me to worry about what people will think?

Bollum: Of course! What people think is important. You don't
            want people to think you are weird. If anybody
            caught you sitting and staring at a white wall ... what
            would they think???

Bollum talks to Barbara – about making an impression

Bollum: You can't go meet such an important person looking
            like that!

Barbara: Looking like what?

Bollum: Like you look!

Barbara: What do you mean?

Bollum: Well you're wearing your old jeans and a sweater to
            begin with! And not very much make-up.

Barbara: What's wrong with my old jeans and a sweater—and
            with not wearing much make-up?

Bollum: Well you want to make a good impression don't you?

Barbara: What do my jeans and sweater and make-up have to
            do with making a good impression?

Bollum: Oh come on Barbara. You know you need to look "hip
            and trendy" to make an impression. Everyone knows
            that!

Barbara: Really? I thought people were interested in
            the energy you radiate and whether or not your
            presence is uplifting, loving and positive...

Bollum: I don't know about that, all I know is you'd definitely
            make a better impression if you were wearing your
            Armani jeans instead of your old Levis!

Barbara: You might be right, but if that's the case, I'm not sure I
            want to make such a good impression. If all people
            care about is my clothes and my make-up... well who
            needs it!

Bollum: But you've got to be realistic girl! That's the way the
            world is... I'm just trying to help you be a success out
            there...

Barbara: You are always talking about being a success... what about having integrity and being honest?

Bollum: Well that might sound good—but how far will it get you in this world?

Barbara: Well I don't know, but I'm sure going to give it a try.

Bollum: You're hopeless, hopeless! With your attitude, you might as well say goodbye to fame and fortune forever! I'm going shopping! Maybe I'll be able to find some decent clothes for you now that the sales are on!

Bollum talks to Barbara – about meeting people

Bollum: Barbara you really need to get out there and meet some new people.

Barbara: Really?

Bollum: Yeah girl, you can't just sit here by yourself all the time.

Barbara: I can't...

Bollum: No girl, you got to be social. You know. You got to get out there and meet people.

Barbara: I do?

Bollum: Yeah you do... Otherwise you'll never be happy.

Barbara: What does meeting other people have to do with being happy?

Bollum: Oh come on dear, you know that human beings are social animals.

Barbara: Do I?

Bollum: Sometimes you are so dense. Didn't you learn in school the importance of making friends and networking? That's what keeps society together.

Barbara: No I can't remember learning anything like that in school. In fact, I can't remember learning anything in school at all.

Bollum: Oh yeah, I forgot, you went to school in America. And all you do there is memorize stuff for tests. Well anyway, here in Denmark where you now live, people learn the importance of socializing.

Barbara: They do? I don't find the Danes very social.

Bollum: No, you're right. Maybe that's why they teach it in school here. But we're getting off the subject. I just wanted to point out to you that you can't just sit on your sofa all day long and bliss out, you've got to get out there and meet people if you want to be happy.

Barbara: But I'm perfectly happy sitting on my sofa blissing out as you call it. What can other people give me that I don't already have?

Bollum: What can other people give you? Well they can give you happiness you jerk!

Barbara: Happiness? You mean that I need other people to be happy?

Bollum: Obviously. No one can be happy without other people.

Barbara: Really? That's an interesting thought. But is it true?

Bollum: Of course it's true.

Barbara: Well not in my experience. I've been with other people lots of times and felt absolutely miserable.

Bollum: Well that's your own fault my dear. You've got to learn to compromise and do what other people want you to do if you're going to be happy when you're with other people.

Barbara: Exactly... so why would I want to do that when I'm already perfectly happy sitting on my sofa blissing out all by myself. I don't need to compromise with anybody about anything to do that.

Bollum: Look I've got this great idea for you. I've just found this fantastic dating site for you on the Internet.

Barbara: Really?

Bollum: Yeah really. All you have to do is go online and I'm sure you'll meet all these fantastic men you can hang out with.

Barbara: And why would I want to do that? I'm still recovering from my last disastrous relationship!

Bollum: I know, but you've got to move on and have fun!

Barbara: But I am having fun sitting here on my sofa just blissing out.

Bollum: Look Barbara... all you have to do is click here... it's really easy...

Bollum talks to Barbara – about making a plan

Bollum: Barbara, you've got to take control of your life girl!

Barbara: Really?

Bollum: Yes really! What a question! If you don't take control, things will get out of hand.

Barbara: Really? Is it true?

Bollum: Of course it's true my precious. You have to get a grip and take charge of your life.

Barbara: I do?

Bollum: Of course you do.

Barbara: So what do you suggest?

Bollum: Well first of all you have to make a plan.

Barbara: A plan?

Bollum: You have to have a clear goal and make a plan on how to achieve it.

Barbara: Really? I'm doing just fine the way I am.

Bollum: Oh come on girl. Without a plan—without a clear roadmap as to how you are going to move forward in life—you'll never get anywhere.

Barbara: But why would I want to go anywhere? I'm perfectly happy right where I am.

Bollum: How can you be perfectly happy right now? No one knows you, you're not famous or rich or anything. You're just a middle-aged woman who likes to lie on her sofa a lot. You're an absolute nothing.

Barbara: Well it's true I'm not rich or famous or anything and I do like to lie on my sofa a lot, feeling perfectly happy! So I can't see why I need a plan.

Bollum: Well a plan will help you go somewhere.

Barbara: But I just told you, I don't want to go anywhere.

Bollum: You seem to think everything's perfect right here.

Barbara: Yes that's true. Everything is perfect right here.

Bollum: Well I don't see it!

Barbara: Obviously you don't see it but I do!

Bollum: What's so perfect about this moment?

Barbara: What's not so perfect about this moment?

Bollum: Well you could have more.

Barbara: More of what?

Bollum: More of everything!

Barbara: And why would I want more of everything?

Bollum: Because then you'd be happy!

Barbara: But I told you I'm already happy!

Bollum: But how can you be happy with so little?

Barbara: What does "having stuff" have to do with happiness?

Bollum: Well you have to "have stuff" to be happy, everyone knows that.

Barbara: Really? That's not my experience. In my experience, happiness is what I am.

Bollum: Oh now you've really lost me...

Barbara: Obviously!

Bollum talks to Barbara – about being single

Bollum: Everyone knows it's better to be in a relationship than to be single.

Barbara: They do?

Bollum: Of course. Why do you think everyone's trying to find a partner?

Barbara: I just read that 51% of the women in the US are now single. So there are more single women in the US than

	there are women in relationships... and there are 1,000,000 singles in Denmark (with a population of 5,000,000) and 200,000 singles in Copenhagen alone...
Bollum:	Well just think how many women there are out there who are trying to find partners! It must be great for single men!
Barbara:	Well what if they don't want partners?
Bollum:	But of course they do.
Barbara:	All 51% of them?
Bollum:	Yes all 51% of them...
Barbara:	You mean to say there isn't one woman out there who is happy being single?
Bollum:	I doubt it very much.
Barbara:	But you can't know for sure can you?
Bollum:	Well I guess not—but how can anyone be single and happy at the same time?
Barbara:	Well I'm single and pretty happy...
Bollum:	Oh you... but you're so weird Barbara, you know that?
Barbara:	Really? So I'm weird because I'm single and sometimes happy!
Bollum:	Definitely. No one can find happiness without another person.
Barbara:	But is that true?
Bollum:	Absolutely.
Barbara:	Well if what you are saying is true, it means that millions of women (and men too) are doomed to unhappiness for the rest of their lives because they don't have a partner.
Bollum:	Yup! That's why I keep telling you to go online and find a partner, Barbara. It's important for your happiness!
Barbara:	So what you are really saying is that my happiness depends on someone else?
Bollum:	Yup that's exactly what I'm saying!

Barbara: And that my happiness has nothing to do with me?

Bollum: Well a little... I mean you've got to be a sweet person too...

Barbara: Oh... so now you're saying my happiness has a little bit to do with me...

Bollum: Well sometimes... but now you're twisting my words around. I just want you to go out there and meet a man and have some fun girl!

Barbara: But why do I need a man to have fun?

Bollum: Oh sometimes you are so dense girl—don't you read the women's magazines? You've got to have a man to have fun, that's all they write about... pick up any magazine and you'll see what I'm talking about...

Barbara: Yeah that's why I don't read women's magazines... I don't want my happiness ruined by their ridiculous ideas... they don't know what they're talking about as far as I can see. My happiness depends on what's going on in my head—not on any man...

Bollum: Oh there you go again with all this mind stuff. No wonder no man wants to be with you!

Barbara: What do you mean by that?

Bollum: Well you're always saying that your happiness is up to you...

Barbara: Well it is...

Bollum: Well what man could live with that! Men want women to make them happy! Any idiot knows that!

Barbara: Yeah... which is exactly why I don't want to hang out with most men...

Bollum: Oh you're hopeless... hopeless...

Barbara: Yeah me and all the rest of us single women!

Bollum talks to Barbara – about the financial crisis

Bollum: It's just terrible. I don't know what we're going to do!

Barbara: About what?

Bollum:	About the financial crisis, you nitwit… don't you read the newspapers?
Barbara:	Yes, I do read the newspapers…
Bollum:	Well then you should know, this is a very serious situation, we could starve.
Barbara:	Really?
Bollum:	Yes my dear… STARVE!
Barbara:	Well last time I looked (5 minutes ago), I had plenty of food in my refrigerator.
Bollum:	Oh I'm not talking about now silly! I'm talking about the future.
Barbara:	Oh I see. Well I don't know about the future.
Bollum:	Obviously, that's why I think we need a plan.
Barbara:	A plan for what?
Bollum:	A plan to survive.
Barbara:	Oh so you think we can make a plan to survive the financial crisis?
Bollum:	Of course we can.
Barbara:	Really? Well what do you think we should do Mr. WiseGuy—go out and force people to buy my books at gunpoint?
Bollum:	Now you're just being silly.
Barbara:	Well what do you mean?
Bollum:	Well first of all, you've got to start by saving.
Barbara:	Really? What should I save? I don't buy anything to begin with.
Bollum:	Well you know, cut down on frivolous stuff like expensive make-up and designer clothes and travels to exotic places… you know.
Barbara:	Well I don't use expensive makeup or wear designer clothes or go on exotic travels to begin with… you know that… according to you all I do is bliss out on my sofa…
Bollum:	Hmm.

Barbara: So what else can I do?

Bollum: You know this makes me really worried. There must be something you can cut down on?

Barbara: I'm sure there is.

Bollum: But you know the danger is with everyone cutting down on their consumption the whole economy will come to a standstill...

Barbara: Well that's what they say but you know I was thinking that this slowdown must be good for the environment... you know with everyone consuming less...

Bollum: Oh come on!

Barbara: No I'm serious. Just think about how good this is for the environment. Factories are making less so there's less waste and less CO_2 emission and people are buying fewer cars and travelling less so there's less CO_2 emission and...

Bollum: I never thought about that...

Barbara: Well maybe you should. Maybe this so-called financial crisis is Mother Earth's way of making a much needed adjustment.

Bollum: Really?

Barbara: Well if we can't cut down on our ridiculous over-consumption and stop trashing the planet by ourselves, maybe Mother Earth is doing it for us.

Bollum: But what about all the people who are out of work and who might starve?

Barbara: Well maybe that's Mother Earth's way of telling us to get our act together and start taking better care of the planet and of each other too... instead of just reading fashion magazines and thinking about ourselves...

Bollum: Oh there you go again...

Bollum talks to Barbara – about making more money (again)!

Bollum:	You should be making more money Barbara.
Barbara:	That's what you said last week.
Bollum:	But it's true, you should.
Barbara:	More money than what?
Bolllum:	More money that you're making right now stupid!
Barbara:	But I'm not.
Bollum:	I noticed and it sucks.
Barbara:	What sucks?
Bollum:	The fact that you're not making more money.
Barbara:	Like how does it suck?
Bollum:	Well we could starve.
Barbara:	You said that before too.
Bollum:	Well nothing's changed and the world economy is going to the dogs!
Barbara:	You said that before too.
Bollum:	But you're obviously not listening... I want you to listen!
Barbara:	I am listening and you're giving me a headache!
Bollum:	Well it's important!
Barbara:	Is it important to give me a headache?
Bollum:	No stupid, listening to me is important!
Barbara:	Why is listening to you important, you're driving me crazy.
Bollum:	Well if you listen to me you might do something!
Barbara:	I was doing something!
Bollum:	Like what?
Barbara:	I was having a good time.
Bollum:	A good time—when the world is going under!
Barbara:	Everything looks fine to me.
Bollum:	You're hopeless... If only I could talk some sense into you.
Barbara:	Your idea of sense gives me a headache.

Bollum: But life isn't a dance on roses my dear.

Barbara: No?

Bollum: Now stop being silly will you?

Barbara: I'm not being silly. Life looks pretty good to me... as far as I can see.

Bollum: You must be totally blind. Can't you see what's going on?

Barbara: Yes perfectly. I was sitting here having a perfectly good time until you showed up.

Bollum: Now you're insulting my intelligence!

Barbara: Well what's so intelligent about wanting me to overlook the beauty of this moment?

Bollum: You can't just live on this moment.

Barbara: Really? I didn't know there was any other option!

Bollum: Of course there is girl. You've got to be serious and make plans.

Barbara: I am serious and my plan is to be here now and enjoy the beauty of this moment.

Bollum: But a plan like that will get you nowhere.

Barbara: And where exactly should I go.

Bollum: Forward silly!

Barbara: Forward?

Bollum: You know, make more money so we'll be secure and happy tomorrow.

Barbara: What about being secure and happy right now!

Bollum: You can't live forever on that!

Barbara: Are you sure?

Bollum talks to Barbara – about finding a new relationship

Bollum: The guy you went out with the other night seems like a pretty nice man Barbara.

Barbara: Yes he was OK.

Bollum: Well that's great.

Barbara: Why is that great?

Bollum: Because now you have someone you can be in a relationship with!

Barbara: A relationship? Why would I want to be in a relationship with someone like him?

Bollum: Well you just said he was nice.

Barbara: What does nice have to do with it?

Bollum: Well you have to be with someone!

Barbara: I do?

Bollum: Yes woman. You can't spend the rest of your life living alone.

Barbara: Really. Why not?

Bollum: Well it's scary to live alone, you know that.

Barbara: What's scary about living alone? I thought it was even more scary living *with* someone the last time I tried it!

Bollum: But that was your own fault woman. You were too stubborn, hanging on to your career and ideas like you did. You know you have to make compromises if you live with a man. You just can't have everything your way.

Barbara: So I noticed.

Bollum: Yes you have to compromise if you want it to work.

Barbara: But is that really true?

Bollum: Of course it's really true. Everyone knows that. You have to give up a lot of things to live in a relationship. How many times have I told you that?

Barbara: Well why would I want to do that? Give up the things that are important to me?

Bollum: Because that's what people do.

Barbara: I can see that, but why would I want to do that?

Bollum: Because like I said, you can't go on living alone.

Barbara: Why not?

Bollum: Well how will you manage?

Barbara: Manage? What do you mean by that? I pay my rent don't I? And buy my own food. What does that have to do with being in a relationship?

Bollum: Well that's OK for now, but what if something serious happens? Who is going to take care of you then?

Barbara: What about me?

Bollum: Well what if you can't take care of yourself?

Barbara: Well I have friends and family and I live in a country where there is a support system for people who can't take care of themselves.

Bollum: I know, but that's not the same as someone who loves you.

Barbara: But isn't that love?

Bollum: Hmm… well maybe it is, but that's not the kind of love I was talking about. I was talking about the "man-woman" type of love silly. The kind of love that knocks you off your feet. You know the "one and only" kind of love that they sing about in the love songs. You know the kind of love that really breaks your heart when it's gone!

Barbara: Oh that kind. Yeah I've tried that kind of love and it always makes me feel like I can't breathe…

Bollum: Sometimes I just don't understand you. You and your freedom! Can't you see that if you had that kind of love, you'd be willing to sacrifice everything for it?

Barbara: Really?

Bollum: Yes really, with a man like that in your life, you could give up your career and everything and just let him take care of you for the rest of your life.

Barbara: And why would I want to do that? Why would I want to give up my career and everything that's important to me for a man?

Bollum: Because that's what women do silly!

Barbara: I know but it sure doesn't sound like love to me, it sounds more like suicide!

Bollum talks to Barbara – about improving this moment

Bollum: There are so many things you could do to improve this moment Barbara.

Barbara: Really? Like what?

Bollum: Well you could clean up the apartment and wash your hair and sort out the papers in your office and...

Barbara: Hold it, hold it, just hold it for a moment.

Bollum: And pay your bills and get ready for work tomorrow...

Barbara: Hold it, hold it... will you please!

Bollum: And exercise and ...

Barbara: Will you please just give me a moment to say something.

Bollum: OK well what?

Barbara: OK well what does any of that have to do with improving this moment?

Bollum: Well improving yourself and your life is what this moment is for silly.

Barbara: Really?

Bollum: Yes really. What else could it be for?

Barbara: Well what about enjoying this moment for what it is?

Bollum: Oh there you go again.

Barbara: What do you mean?

Bollum: There you go again with all your talk about enjoying the beauty of this moment.

Barbara: Well what's wrong with that?

Bollum: A lot. I mean what's so great about this moment?

Barbara: A lot.

Bollum: Like what?

Barbara: Like for example we're alive and this is it.

Bollum: Well you'll be alive in the future and then that will be it.

Barbara: Can you be sure about that?

Bollum: Well hopefully for your sake!

Barbara: You're always pushing me and trying to get me to get all worked up about tomorrow. Why can't you ever get all worked up about today?

Bollum: Because today is so boring.

Barbara: Really?

Bollum: Yeah. The now is so boring, but tomorrow—well tomorrow will be just great if only you'd get busy preparing yourself for it.

Barbara: Really? It seems to me I've spent my whole life preparing for tomorrow and now I want to enjoy today.

Bollum: But what about success? What about getting fit? What about making your home a showcase? What about finding a man? What about...

Barbara: Yeah what about it? And what about now? What about this moment? What about just slowing down a bit and breathing into this moment? What about noticing the abundance and fullness of *this*! And *this*. And *this*!

Bollum: Yeah yeah yeah, there you go again. What good is anything of *this* going to do us? Can you tell me that?

Barbara: What good, well *this* is the Good! *This* is the Good I'm seeking. It's right here.

Bollum: You are hopeless! Hopeless! What am I going to do with you?

Barbara: Hopefully nothing!

Bollum: Yeah... nothing. How can you be satisfied with so little?

Barbara: What do you mean? I have so much right now. In fact I have everything. All the wealth of the world belongs to me. You're just so busy improving yourself that you never notice it!

Bollum: Look sweetheart, I just want you to be happy.

Barbara: But I am happy! That's what I've been trying to tell

	you all along!
Bollum:	But how can you be happy without a man and without being a success and without having money in the bank and without...
Barbara:	What does any of that have to do with being happy?
Bollum:	HELP!

Suggested reading

Bhaghavad Gita

Byron Katie
Loving What Is
I Need Your Love – Is That True?
A Thousand Names for Joy
Question Your Thinking, Change the World
Who Would You Be Without Your Story?

Catherine Ponder
The Dynamic Laws of Healing
The Dynamic Laws of Prosperity

David R. Hawkins
Truth VS Falsehood
Discovery of the Presence of God
The Eye of the I from Which Nothing Is Hidden
Healing and Recovery

Deepak Chopra
The Seven Spiritual Laws of Success
Creating Affluence
Power, Freedom and Grace

Dhammapada (Buddha)

Eckhart Tolle
The Power of Now

Stillness Speaks
A New Earth

Eknath Easwaran
Gandhi the Man, the Story of His Transformation

Emma Curtis Hopkins
Scientific Christian Mental Practice

Emmet Fox
Power through Constructive Thinking

Ernest Holmes
Living the Science of Mind

Manuel J. Smith
When I Say No, I Feel Guilty

Mary Baker Eddy
Science and Health

Sogyal Rinpoche
The Tibetan Book of Living and Dying

Sri Nisargadatta Maharaj
I Am That

Stephen Mitchell
Tao Te Ching
The Second Book of the Tao

Steve Hagen
Buddhism Plain and Simple
Meditation Now or Never

Sushila Blackman
Graceful Exits, How Great Beings Die

Barbara Berger
The Road to Power – Fast Food for the Soul
The Road to Power 2 – More Fast Food for the Soul
Gateway to Grace – Barbara Berger's Guide to User-Friendly Meditation
Mental Technology (The 10 Mental Laws) – Software for Your Hardware
The Spiritual Pathway
Are You Happy Now? 10 Ways to Live a Happy Life
Single for the Second Time – The Adventures of Pebble Beach

Tim Ray
Starbrow – A Spiritual Adventure – book 1
Starwarrior – A Spiritual Thriller – book 2
101 Myths About Relationships That Drive Us Crazy – And A Little About What You Can Do About Them

For more information about
Barbara Berger and Tim Ray's
books and activities,
see www.beamteam.com

BOOKS

O is a symbol of the world, of oneness and unity. In different cultures it also means the "eye," symbolizing knowledge and insight. We aim to publish books that are accessible, constructive and that challenge accepted opinion, both that of academia and the "moral majority."

Our books are available in all good English language bookstores worldwide. If you don't see the book on the shelves ask the bookstore to order it for you, quoting the ISBN number and title. Alternatively you can order online (all major online retail sites carry our titles) or contact the distributor in the relevant country, listed on the copyright page.

See our website **www.o-books.net** for a full list of over 500 titles, growing by 100 a year.

And tune in to myspiritradio.com for our book review radio show, hosted by June-Elleni Laine, where you can listen to the authors discussing their books.

MySpiritRadio